Sandra Sider | Foreword by Meg Cox

QUARANTINE QUILTS

Creativity in the
Midst of Chaos

SCHIFFER
PUBLISHING®

4880 Lower Valley Road • Atglen, PA 19310

Other Schiffer Books by the Author:

Exploring Your Artistic Voice in Contemporary Quilt Art,
ISBN 978-0-7643-5887-6

Art Quilts Unfolding: 50 Years of Innovation, Sandra Sider, ed., Nancy
Bavor, Lisa Ellis, Martha Sielman, SAQA (Studio Art Quilt Associates,
Inc.), ISBN 978-0-7643-5626-1

Deeds Not Words: Celebrating 100 Years of Women's Suffrage,
Sandra Sider & Pamela Weeks, ISBN 978-0-7643-5917-0

Other Schiffer Books on Related Subjects:

Quilts of Valor: A 50-State Salute, Quilts of Valor Foundation,
ISBN 978-0-7643-5630-8

Art Quilts International: Abstract & Geometric, Martha Sielman,
ISBN 978-0-7643-5220-1

World War II Quilts, 2nd Edition, Sue Reich, ISBN 978-0-7643-5334-5

Designed by Molly Shields
Cover design by Ashley Millhouse
Front jacket/cover art: Detail, *Quarantined: View from My Window* by Anne Bellas.
Back jacket/cover art: (*clockwise from top left*) Details of *Dandelion: Tough as the
Tooth of a Lion* by Sandra Sider; *Gaslighter in Chief* by Mel Dugosh; *Cinque Terre*
by Roderick Daniel; *Emozioni altalenanti* by Giovanna Nicolai; *Dancing with My
Heart in the Garden of Life* by Shelley Worsham; *Under Siege* by Amanda Bauer;
Kintsukuroi Illuminated by Julie Haddrick.
Type set in Brandon Grotesque / ZapfEllipt BT

ISBN: 978-0-7643-6201-9
Printed in China

Published by Schiffer Publishing, Ltd.
4880 Lower Valley Road
Atglen, PA 19310
Phone: (610) 593-1777; Fax: (610) 593-2002
E-mail: Info@schifferbooks.com
Web: www.schifferbooks.com

For our complete selection of fine books on this and related subjects, please visit
our website at www.schifferbooks.com. You may also write for a free catalog.

Schiffer Publishing's titles are available at special discounts for bulk purchases for
sales promotions or premiums. Special editions, including personalized covers,
corporate imprints, and excerpts, can be created in large quantities for special
needs. For more information, contact the publisher.

We are always looking for people to write books on new and related subjects. If
you have an idea for a book, please contact us at proposals@schifferbooks.com.

"There is a loneliness that can be rocked."

—TONI MORRISON, *Beloved*

CONTENTS

FOREWORD

by Meg Cox

When the call for entries of quarantine quilts went out in early April 2020, the response to the concept was decidedly mixed. Some on social media argued that it was "too soon," that quilts pumped out for a challenge timed for a fall exhibition (later canceled) couldn't possibly capture the deeper currents of the moment. A few even suggested it was disrespectful of the sick and dying, trivializing a growing global pandemic to focus on quilts.

But the dozens of quilters all over the world who immediately responded to Sandra's request felt strongly otherwise. Many were already deep into the creative process on their own, looking for both a respite from the plague and a place to express their difficult experiences and worries in a soft, safe, forgiving medium. Having the three-month deadline only helped them focus harder, and know they were not alone in this urge.

There is little doubt that COVID-19 will inspire artists, quilt makers included, for a long time to come. But if anthropologists want to understand the lives and feelings of people around the world at the chaotic start of the pandemic, these visceral, heat-of-the-moment quilts will be a valuable guide.

The nearly one hundred quilts in this book selected out of more than two hundred entered in the *Quarantine Quilts* challenge show how contradictory the experience was, even within one quilter's life. Many artists' narratives depict the opposition between the terror and anxiety they felt about the rising infection and death rates versus the relative peace and quiet they felt while quilting.

In future years, when I take down this book and dive into these visual responses to the hard times I shared, so many memories of my own quarantine will return. Especially the jarring juxtaposition of extreme fear and uncertainty with unexpected joy in the surprising ways my narrowed world deepened. Although I don't have a specific pandemic-themed quilt to show for those early months, I'll remember how time stopped as I stitched mask after mask in my basement studio. And how time spent working on quilts and other projects kept me mindful of all the things I could accomplish, instead of all the things I couldn't.

I'm grateful to Sandra Sider for capturing and preserving this fraught global unraveling in fixed threads.

Meg Cox is a nationally known thought leader on the topics of quilting and family traditions. www.megcox.com

PREFACE

"I shunned the face of man; all sound of joy or complacency was torture to me; solitude was my only consolation—deep, dark, death-like solitude."

—Mary Shelley,
Frankenstein

It was on March 1, 2020, that the first person in New York City, my home, tested positive for the novel coronavirus. Within a week, after seventy-six cases of COVID-19 had been reported, a state of emergency was declared across the state by Governor Cuomo. Only seven days later, on March 14, there were 613 cases in the state and two deaths. That was the day I drove away from New York City with my husband and several boxes of books and art supplies to reside indefinitely in our summerhouse in the mountains of northeastern Pennsylvania. Upon arriving, we put ourselves into quarantine for fourteen days, to make sure that we were not bringing the contagion into our community. Two days later, Governor Cuomo closed the New York schools statewide, and the entire state was put on "PAUSE" as of March 20, including a stay-at-home order. In late March, most residents of New York City went into self-quarantine as they realized that the city was becoming the national epicenter of the contagion.

As I began writing this essay at the end of May 2020, New York City remained the only part of the state still on PAUSE. More than 16,000 city residents had died from the virus, and many thousands of "non-essential" New Yorkers were living in isolation for more than two months—many of them in hardship conditions that made my quarantine seem like an extended spring vacation. This extreme living situation lasted almost as long for millions of people around the globe, and the future remains extremely uncertain as coronavirus spikes and surges continue as of this writing, and the world attempts to cope with the ongoing impacts.

After we arrived in Pennsylvania during a very chilly March, I set up a makeshift studio and sat in front of my work tables, reeling from the sudden dis-location, confused about what was happening at the national level, and attempting to accept the fact that our lives were topsy-turvy, with no end in sight of canceled travel and no way to visit our family in California or plan anything—except for what I could control, such as an art project and the seemingly end-less parade of desserts being baked in our kitchen.

The impetus to begin making something was almost a compulsion, and I wondered whether other makers were feeling the same, and whether I might somehow document their work during isolation and maybe even encourage them. Since my medium is studio art quilts, I contacted Karey Bresenhan about possibly having a *Quarantine Quilts* call for entry resulting in an exhi-bition at the 2020 Houston International Quilt Festival. I also reached out to Sandra Korinchak, my editor at Schiffer Publishing, about having a 2021 book titled *Quarantine Quilts: Creativity in the Midst of Chaos*. They both enthusiastically supported these dual projects, and within two weeks I began hearing from other artists about what they were making. All twen-ty-seven works selected for the Houston exhibition are presented in this book, plus seventy others, along with a few examples of *The Quarantine Quilt* blocks for a monumental community quilt organized by the Wisconsin Museum of Quilts and Fiber Arts—one of several such projects worldwide and one of the first to invite participants.

My concept for this book goes beyond documenting quilts made in isolation because I also wanted to share how makers reacted to and perhaps were inspired by working in quarantine. Narratives of isolation contex-tualize the artwork published in this book and imbue it with deeper meaning. The lonely artist struggling in a garret is a stereotype with which we all are famil-iar, but that artist was able to go out to a café or party with friends when the mood struck. Not a single maker in this book had that freedom, being forced to stay inside in order to stay alive, and possibly save the lives of others. They range from retired quilters living alone with a huge stash of fabric, to parents of small children juggling family commitments, nervous about possible food insecurity, and having no private space for themselves or the usual materials with which to make quilts. At times the emotion of fear has been palpable, with the very air we breathe carrying illness and possibly death.

The relentless sameness of the days forced us to turn inward, relying on our individual psyches to survive—a truly transformative experience that none of us ever expected. Making something with our hands—a garden, cake, sweater, birdhouse, game for the children, newly painted room, or work of art—in-volves a process that we can control, leading to a sense of purpose and satisfaction, of meaningful moments in what has become a chaotic, unpredictable world.

INTRODUCTION

What History Has Taught Us

Human beings have endured waves of devastating epidemic and pandemic illnesses since prehistoric times, more than five thousand years ago. Three such illnesses killed millions of people across Europe during antiquity, and bubonic plague swept through the Byzantine Empire during the sixth century. Seven years of the so-called Black Death from Asia to Europe in the fourteenth century changed the entire culture of Europe, similar to what seems to be happening today worldwide due to COVID-19. During the sixteenth century, a type of hemorrhagic fever devastated Mexico and Central America, while simultaneously perhaps as much as 90 percent of the indigenous populations of the Americas and Caribbean islands were killed by smallpox and other epidemic diseases introduced from Europe.

London lost 15 percent of its population in the 1660s due to bubonic plague, Marseilles lost as many as 30 percent of its residents in the early eighteenth century, and Moscow may have lost as much as 60 percent of its people owing to plague in the 1770s. The late eighteenth century witnessed the first epidemic of yellow fever in the United States, as Philadelphia suffered a horrific death rate owing to this mosquito-borne infection, with many thousands of residents in other port cities dying of yellow fever during the nineteenth century. As a result of transport via steamship and aggressive colonization in the nineteenth century, cholera swept into several areas of the world. It remains a serious epidemic threat today in regions where continuous supplies of clean, fresh water are unavailable.

Toward the close of the nineteenth century, the first worldwide pandemic of influenza infected millions, partly owing to transmission via rail transport—a preview of the COVID-19 transmission via air travel. During the past 250 years, the world has experienced at least ten major epidemics due to a type of influenza. Epidemics of polio, a strain of virus infecting the spinal cord, terrified parents of small children from 1916 until the 1950s, when a vaccine was invented. The fear of polio is remembered well by several makers in this book, whose schools closed early in spring and who were unnecessarily forbidden to go swimming out of ignorance about the cause of polio. Children were quarantined in their homes to avoid infection, a memory of isolation that reverberates today for those in their seventies and older.

In 1918, some 500 million people across the globe contracted a powerful strain of pandemic influenza, resulting in unimaginable death tolls of 100 million over more than a year. This is the pandemic most closely compared to COVID-19 because of its global reach and longevity. In the century between this pandemic and COVID-19, the world has witnessed smallpox killing nearly 300 million worldwide; the avian flu of the 1950s killing 116,000 people in the US; the horrific AIDS pandemic of the 1980s—still continuing at an alarming rate in some parts of the world; the swine flu of 2009 infecting 1.4 billion people; the Ebola epidemic of 2014, from which more than 11,000 people in Africa died; 10.4 million new cases worldwide of tuberculosis each year; the ongoing epidemic of the Zika virus so devastating to unborn infants; and finally, COVID-19, a deadly type of SARS virus.

With the horror of COVID-19 continuing to spike across the United States and elsewhere, much of the world has become frustrated and debilitated by shutdowns, lockdowns, and the prospect of renewed quarantines. History, however, has taught us that the human spirit can be amazingly resilient, creative, and even inspiring, in spite of and sometimes because of isolation—whether we are physically separated from other people for various reasons, such as imprisonment or spiritual pursuits, or forced into quarantine alone or with friends and family for protection from disease, which is our situation due to COVID-19. History has also taught us that epidemic and pandemic diseases are part of the human condition, that we should have been much better prepared to deal with them, and people everywhere may have to adjust to the new reality of COVID-19 for a long time.

In ancient Greece, epidemic contagion ran rampant through Athens between 430 and 425 BCE, when the city-state was at war with Sparta during the Peloponnesian War. The historian Thucydides did not let the contagion hinder his work on that drawn-out conflict, and as part of his opus he began documenting the disease's symptoms and possible causes. He himself fell ill but survived, recognizing that being exposed to someone who was ill could transmit the disease. His text is the earliest extant firsthand account of an epidemic, showing an admirable degree of logic, the inquisitive interest of a historian, and creative focus as a writer in the midst of such a crisis.

"The isolation spins its mysterious cocoon, focusing the mind on one place, one time, one rhythm—the turning of the light."

—M. L. Stedman,
The Light Between Oceans

Perhaps the most well-known literary work of the Western world concerning quarantine is the *Decameron* of Giovanni Boccaccio, a book of lively tales supposedly told over ten days by a group of young people who escaped from Florence, Italy, to quarantine themselves in a villa several miles away. Boccaccio lived through the Black Death of 1348 in Florence, which killed half the city's population, including members of his family. The *Decameron's* introduction relates the horror and chaos of a city in the grip of an uncontrollable epidemic. But the stories that follow, all told in a beautiful garden, are clever, sexy, and occasionally humorous. We can imagine Boccaccio as placing himself in that garden, mentally distanced from the devastation of Florence.

2020 Quarantine Art Projects

The internet has made it possible not only for individuals to share their quarantine projects, but also for collaborative and community art projects to flourish. Many of the results consist of digital art, especially photography, while some are handmade, such as the quilts in this book, with others being artwork made by hand by numerous individuals and then reformatted digitally into an installation, either in a museum setting or online.

South African artist Zanele Muholi photographed herself during lockdown wearing masks and gloves, Kara Walker has been working through her emotional reactions to COVID-19 isolation with a series of drawings, and British sculptor Wilfrid Wood made a hyper-realistic bust portrait of himself, longing to show his work in the tangible world. These are just a few of the hundreds of individual quarantine works of art published online and in print to illustrate articles about our current crisis. While not all of the artwork directly addresses the coronavirus as a subject, the makers discuss their situations with varying degrees of introspection.

In several instances, the frustration of isolation in 2020 led to remarkable creativity, one of the most innovative examples being Australian dancer Ashleigh Perrie, who has some experience in costume designing.

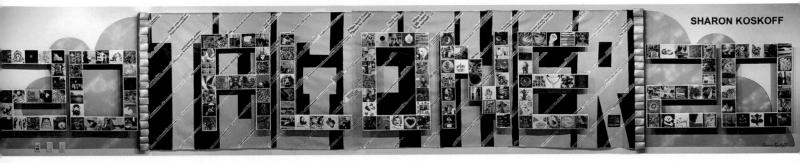

SHARON KOSKOFF

ALONE TOGETHER: *A Corona Crisis Collage . . . the Socially Distant Mural Installation.* Displayed at the Cultural Council for Palm Beach County in Lake Worth, Florida. Photo: Sharon Koskoff, who organized the project.
A is for Antiviral medications and Antibodies that may save us
L is always for Love
O is to keep your mask ON!
N is the New Normal
E is for Education, Emergency, Empathy, and my Extended family

She was working on the MS *Zaandam* cruise ship while it was stuck at sea for sixty days, not permitted to dock anywhere, with multiple quarantines and lockdowns. Finally arriving home via plane from The Netherlands, she was strictly quarantined for fourteen days in a hotel in Perth—a traveler's COVID homecoming experienced by thousands of people worldwide. Her meals were served in large paper bags, with disposable cutlery and dishes. As the bags began to pile up, they inspired Perrie to begin manipulating them to design outfits for herself, including a tutu, a tennis costume complete with racket and visor, and gowns titled *Origami Diva* and *Queen Quarantina*. Creativity and humor sustained her through fourteen days of isolation.

Probably the most famous worldwide art-related project during our 2020 period of spring quarantine was the Getty Museum's challenge via Twitter to recreate a work of art using only three things lying around the house, along with the people and animals residing there. As reported in early April by Forbes online, the challenge went viral, as many thousands of people submitted their "masterpieces," some of which were eerily accurate and some of which were hilarious. As we might expect, few people observed the "three things" rule in their enthusiasm. Selections from the challenge have been published in a fascinating book titled *Off the Walls*. (This challenge's concept originated with an Instagram account Tussen Kunst & Quarantaine ["Between Art & Quarantine"] and was also posted by the Rijksmuseum in Amsterdam.)

Florida artist Sharon Koskoff sent out a call via Facebook on March 21 for her *Alone Together* monumental mural project, a prime example of how a community art project could succeed during quarantine. With a deadline of April 13, she challenged people to make a piece of art in square format, preferably 6 by 6 inches, sending her a digital photograph of the completed work to incorporate into a "Corona Crisis Collage." The mural, created by Koskoff's printing out the digital images, was installed in the Cultural Council for Palm Beach County in Lake Worth, Florida, with a virtual "opening" on June 13, 2020. It is 5 feet tall and 30 feet wide, featuring 164 squares by 113 Palm Beach County artists.

Koskoff explained, "My goal is to keep all artists productive and working!" (email to the author, June 15, 2020). That was also my goal in assembling this book, specifically for quilt makers in quarantine. Almost all the quilts in this book were begun within the same four-month period in 2020, during Year One of the global pandemic. While the quilts themselves did not necessarily have to be about COVID-19 as a subject, you will find that most of them are.

Let's now turn to these works and their makers' narratives of isolation, beginning with the *Quarantine Quilts* exhibition intended for the 2020 Houston International Quilt Festival. Although that event had to be canceled due to alarming spikes of COVID-19 in Houston, here we can experience this collection of thoughtful and sometimes provocative artwork. The exhibition is now scheduled for summer of 2021 at the National Quilt Museum in Paducah, Kentucky, barring any further closures due to COVID-19.

Quarantine Quilts Exhibition

More than two hundred makers entered quilts for the juried exhibition planned for Houston in 2020, which was also the pool used to select most of the quilts in this book. During the selection process, my goal was to include a variety of themes and styles, staying within the size requirements for the show for Quilts, Inc. at the convention center. Quilts had to be at least 24 inches on the shorter side, no wider than 60 inches, and no taller than 84 inches. Except for a piece by one Canadian artist, all quilts in the exhibition, juried anonymously, happen to be by artists residing in the United States.

For the most part, these quilts fit into the categories of the book itself, beginning with a picturesque stone building by Kathy Menzie where, if you look closely, you will see the coronavirus rolling down the steps toward the viewer. Other circular imagery, such as in the piece by Katie Pasquini Masopust, resonate in our mind's eye with the shape of the virus hammered into our brains by the media. The theme of home is both poignant and ambivalent, from Dorothy's red shoes by Denise Vokoun to Libby Cerullo's exhausted figure in isolation.

Various precautions to stay safe appear in several quilts, including Hope Wilmarth's graffiti-inspired message and Gina Gililland McCasland's colorful graphic lettering. Disrupted patterns and symbolic abstraction are responses to the chaos and confusion of our pandemic lives, yet with some artists finding solace in images of gardens and the imaginary vistas of forbidden travel, such as Teresa Barkley's paean to transportation and communication. Finally, 2020 will forever be remembered by a new movement for social justice sparked by the unforgivable death of George Floyd at the hands of police in Minneapolis, referenced in Miki Rodriguez's quilt. Floyd's dying gasp of "I can't breathe" brought a new meaning to these same words mouthed by the many thousands who have died from COVID-19.

Artists' Narratives

When I found this photo in my collection and coincidently reread Ray Bradbury's 1962 novel *Something Wicked This Way Comes*, I knew I had found a combination that expressed the malaise I have been feeling. The foreboding dark walls and tunnel provide a background for the COVID-19 particle rolling down the stairs. But in spite of the darkness, there is a patch of light, just outside the gate, so hope is not lost.

—*Kathy Menzie*
Topeka, Kansas, USA

During these turbulent times, I wanted to represent the progression of life through dark and light spaces, chaos, the crossing of paths with others, and the sure continuation of life on this planet.

—*Carolyn Maia Burton*
Seattle, Washington, USA

I love to paint, I love to quilt, so having to shelter in place was not such a hardship for me. I have lots of supplies! So much fabric and so many paints that I was very happy to hide away in my studio. I created this piece by painting five different canvases with acrylic paint. Each canvas was a different texture of painting from lines to curves, blocks to grids. I enjoy painting the different panels then cut them up to make this construction based on the circles with the strong striped panel weaving through them. The circle was not intended to represent the virus, but it kind of does. I enjoy all of this free time to work on quilts in my studio, but I do miss my students and traveling to teach. I have a strong "quaranteam" of my sister, cousin, and best friend, and we stay safe so that we can get together occasionally. We all have family that we want to see and keep safe.

—*Katie Pasquini Masopust*
Fortuna, California, USA

I was swirling around inside, not being able to focus those first few weeks in early March 2020. I really needed something tangible to say, "*That* is what I am feeling!" I find quilt making to be the best way to get anxiety out of my body and head. This is my second COVID quarantine quilt because one just wasn't enough to work through all the changes of emotion.

—*Victoria Findlay Wolfe*
New York, New York, USA

OPPOSITE: Kathy Menzie, *Something Wicked This Way Comes*, 32 × 27.5 in.
Collection of Sandra Sider.

Carolyn Maia Burton, *Continuum*, 57.5 × 57.5 in.
Photo: Fred Higgins

Victoria Findlay Wolfe, *Chaos and Uncertainty*, 51 × 47 in.
Quilted by Shelly Pagliai. Photo: Alan Radom

The coronavirus has affected all of us in different ways, from good to bad, causing multiple ripples in our life. This handwork piece was started to give me something to do while binge-watching endless hours of TV since I was stuck at home in quarantine, allowing me time to contemplate how my life has changed or will yet change because of it.

—Amy Clements
Rexburg, Idaho, USA

In creating this quilt, I sought a sense of calmness and safety despite feeling that the world around me was collapsing. Having recently moved to a new state when the pandemic hit, I homed in on my new landscape. I used fabric dyed with bits of rusty metal picked up on land homesteaded by my husband's great-great-grandfather. That family's search for home resonated with me as I underwent what I imagined to be a similar process of emotional adjustment.

—Marika Pineda
Santa Fe, New Mexico, USA

Challenges in life seem overwhelming while we are in the midst of the turmoil, yet we all have had the power within us to make it through. During the COVID-19 quarantine, as I created this quilt, it reminded me: "I've Got the Power in Me" and "There's No Place Like Home!"
(Inspired by a Warner Bros. photograph from *The Wizard of Oz*.)

—Denise Vokoun
Inver Grove Heights, Minnesota, USA

This is number 22 in my series of commemorative quilts. The series began with the 9/11 terrorist attacks. I wanted to design an art quilt that took a different stance from my previous commemorative quilts. With this virus hitting during the spring planting season, I chose to address the topic of growing and spreading. If you look at this artwork through creative eyes, you may see the trellises morph into white cemetery crosses.

—Susan Hoppenworth
Georgetown, Texas, USA

Amy Clements, *The Ripple Effect: Corona Virus*, 24 × 24 in.

Marika Pineda, *Homestead*, 38 × 38 in.

Denise Vokoun, *The Power in Me*, 30.5 × 31 in.

Susan Hoppenworth, *Coronavine*, 29.5 × 27 in.

This quilt evolved from a mis-sized face I had made for another quilt. I was thinking about what I could do with this sad-looking face. Then it came to me that many people were longing now because we are having to shelter in place. I gave the man a coffee cup and added a fogged-up window where he could reflect on what he was feeling.

—*Kay Braunig Donges*
Blairsville, Georgia, USA

Kay Braunig Donges, *Shelter in Place*, 30 × 37 in.

This piece shows a figure facedown on a mountain of frenetic colors and shapes, surrounded by details, data, activities, disorganization, expectations, concerns, and needs. In any crisis or significant life change, there is a point at which I feel overwhelmed. Only rest and self-care restore my brain and body so I can regroup and rally.

—Libby Cerullo
Elverson, Pennsylvania, USA

Even in quarantine, growth keeps springing up wherever it can, like weeds through the sidewalk. My yoga girl is a long-delayed first attempt at collaging. She represents two of my primary tools for keeping balanced these days: yoga and quilting. It's comforting to know that there are always new horizons for both.

—Maggie Ward
Warrenton, Virginia, USA

My quilt is closely based on Peggy Aare's Great Horned Owl pattern. It was started on February 1, just as the pandemic began to explode. Working on this piece was a way to be creative in the midst of chaos and really focus, for at least a few hours, on something besides organizing my staff and coworkers to work from home, and trying to find hand sanitizer.

—Susan Hilsenbeck
Houston, Texas, USA

During times of extreme stress, I speak affirmations offered up as prayer. "Whatever you do, don't panic, pray & be brave" is my go-to sentence when I must focus for survival. Only God can soothe my mental anguish. The reverse side says "kwitchurbeliakin," i.e., quit complaining and sew!

—Gina Gililland McCasland
Lubbock, Texas, USA

Who knew during this unprecedented period in our lifetime that we would be facing a shortage of toilet paper? I never thought in a million years I would get so excited seeing that there was one package left on the shelf. I felt like I won the grand prize!

—Patti Louise Pasteur
Lincoln, Maine, USA

OPPOSITE: Libby Cerullo, *Exhaustion*, 41.5 × 26.5 in.
Photo: John Woodin

OPPOSITE: Maggie Ward, *Sun Salutation*, 33 × 24 in.

Susan Hilsenbeck, *The Owl*, 35 × 32.5 in.

"Wash UR Hands" is graffiti painted on the railway bridge over I-45 South, outside downtown Houston. During the COVID-19 pandemic, it was sprayed over the iconic graffiti "Be Someone" that had been there for many years and known nationwide as a symbol of Houston. The new message is fitting for the times. "Wash UR Hands" was created at the beginning of the quarantine days of Houston's stay-at-home requirement. I found isolation quite lonely, compounded by the death of my husband of fifty-one years just five months earlier. For me, creativity while grieving has been draining, yet a welcome distraction. During quarantine, I challenged myself to use the materials I have on hand. This piece is the latest in my series of art using a stacked letters technique.

—*Hope Wilmarth*
Houston, Texas, USA

Coronavirus—that's all that anyone talks about, reads about, thinks about. People are hoarding. People are self-quarantining and practicing self-distancing. People are afraid. People are wearing masks. People are sick and dying. All I can say is I'm scared and I am creating art about it.

—*Patricia Kumicich*
Naples, Florida, USA

There is nothing more powerful than the written word. As I thought about doing the quilt, I wanted it to speak to those who saw it. Wanting the visual look to be somewhat invisible like COVID-19. You have to find the words in the elongated type I used. I was fortunate to have had access to fabric, so I chose orange text to pop off of the gray background. It is the same gray background we all feel right now every day, as we do not know how long this will last and currently gray shadows follow our daily lives. Time will pass and we will all fold our "quarantine quilts" away, looking for a brighter day for quilters and their families. Stand as tall as the text in the quilt. We all have more quilts to make that will tell our stories!

—*Roderick C. Ferry*
West Des Moines, Iowa, USA

OPPOSITE: Gina Gililland McCasland, *Whatever You Do . . .* , 58.5 × 46.5 in.

Patti Louise Pasteur, *There Was One Left*, 28 × 27 in.

OPPOSITE: Hope Wilmarth, *Wash UR Hands*, 66 × 38 in.
Photo: Rick Wells

OPPOSITE: Patricia Kumicich, *Social Distancing*, 39 × 32 in.

Roderick C. Ferry, *What You Cannot See*, 72 × 59 in.

In anticipation of store closures, I rushed out to my local quilt shop and purchased 15 yards of assorted solid fabrics. I just started random piecing, making blocks, not sure where I was headed. The result was an empty cityscape, devoid of people. I allowed myself the freedom to play during this pandemic! Sheltering in place allowed me to see things from a new perspective.

—*Jan Soules*
Elk Grove, California, USA

I dwell in the silence before I work. I listen. I look and beckon the muse. This only happens when I'm alone. I am most receptive then. The quarantine was the door that opened, again. I walked through.

—*Wen Redmond*
Strafford, New Hampshire, USA

I began this quilt in mid-February 2020, when my province in Canada had just five confirmed cases of COVID-19. As time went on, and the number of cases grew, I found myself using the making of this quilt as a daily escape from the scary and unpredictable. The gentle curves soothed me to cut them. I let my hand decide where the blade would go. Some days the curves were tighter, and other days they were looser, probably reflecting my state of mind that day. By the time I got to quilting, words like "pandemic," "lockdown," and "quarantine" were commonplace. It was a very frightening time, as the world was changing at a rapid pace. Quilting helped me escape all that. Every morning I would steal away down to my sewing room. I would meditate on every single line of stitching as it wound its way along the gentle curves of the piecing, trying to avoid coming too close to another line, very much like two people passing on the sidewalk do now. Quilting so densely on a larger quilt is not something I would normally choose to do, but I was compelled to do so by the anxiety I was feeling at the time. I took that anxiety and stitched it out on this quilt. I call this quilt *A Way Through* because that is precisely what it was for me: a way to get through the early, unpredictable days of this pandemic.

—*Natalie Skinner*
Victoria, British Columbia, Canada

I designed this block years ago. In May 2020, I revisited it and began changing the value arrangement and diagonals—it was mutating! When I combined it in four-patch squares, I had more mutations. So I named it in honor of the current pandemic—a little dark humor in a dark time. The yellow squares honor the use of this color in the Middle Ages and later to indicate contagion.

—*Karen Grace Fisher*
Tucson, Arizona, USA

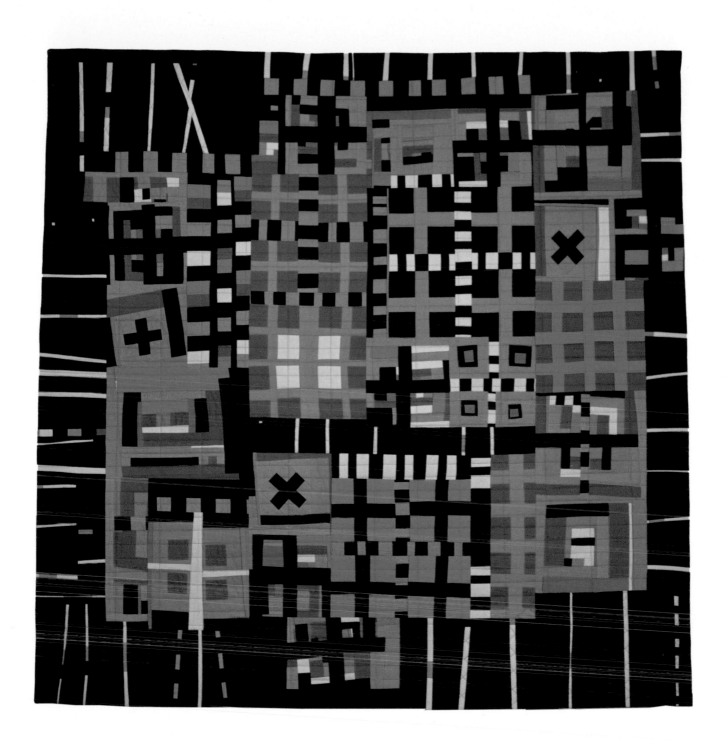

Jan Soules, *Sheltering in Place*, 47 × 46.5 in.

Wen Redmond, *Drawing a Breath*, 22 × 24 in.

Natalie Skinner, *A Way Through*, 59 × 54.5 in.

At the beginning of the shelter-at-home order, I felt flat and uncreative. I eventually pulled out a pile of screen printed and stamped fabric and set myself the task of using them in small compositions. I found great comfort in piecing these quilts, although they became increasingly spiky, reflecting my anxiety about the pandemic. This is the eighth quilt in my COVID-19 series.

—Heather Pregger
Fort Worth, Texas, USA

Especially in the beginning of the quarantine, there were strings of days when I didn't touch my creative work, when the news was all-consuming. I was feeling powerless about the chaos the world seemed to sink into, anxious about the future, and angry about the inadequate governmental response. Being confined at home added feelings of restriction. In addition to sewing face masks for family, friends, and to support a hospital with PPE shortages, the creative process on this quilt helped me to embrace all these feelings and channel them into something creative and positive. Writing my thoughts and feelings down each morning also helped me focus and set my intentions for the day. I used an intuitive and improvisational approach to form the individual geometrical shapes, and later moved them around on the design wall like a puzzle to find the right placement. This creative time demanded complete focus, which allowed me to step away from the chaos in the outside world. With each decision I made on colors and design, I was able to recover a sense of control and agency. *Pandemonium* reflects lessons in patience, accepting imperfections, and coping with anxiety and uncertainty during the quarantine. The final design came together over many weeks as a form of respite and distraction from the constant news stream.

—Lenny van Eijk
Bloomfield, New Jersey, USA

Restrictions due to the COVID-19 pandemic severely limited our daily lives, largely confining us to our homes but allowing more uninterrupted time for creative pursuits. In the midst of our isolation, spring arrived in all its glory, unfettered by human regulation. Plants grew bountifully while birds sang joyously, reminding us of the omnipotent force of nature and providing me with the inspiration for this quilt.

—Geraldine Warner
Wenatchee, Washington, USA

OPPOSITE: Karen Grace Fisher, *COVID 19*, 51 × 45 in.
Quilted by Pamela Golliet on a longarm machine.

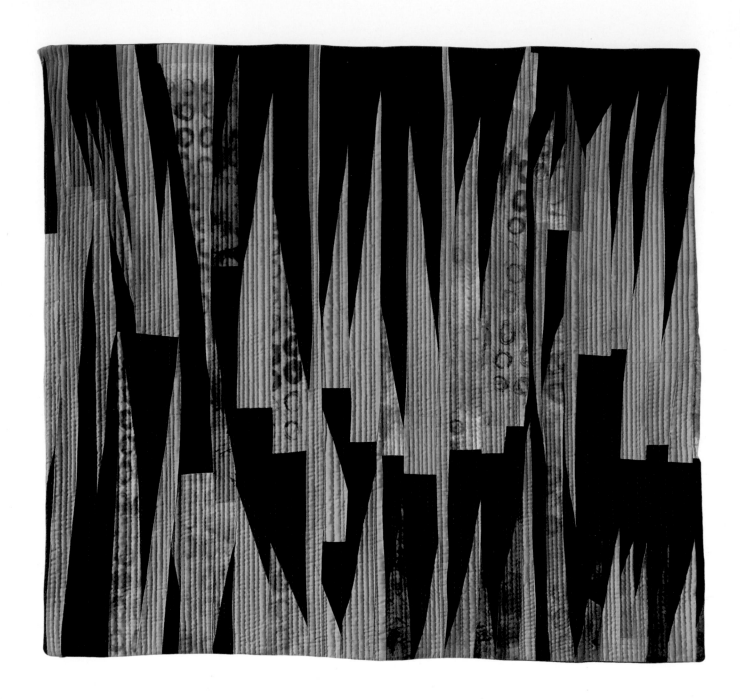

Heather Pregger, *Viral Spike #3*, 26.5 × 28 in.

OPPOSITE: Lenny van Eijk, *Pandemonium*, 45 × 36 in.
Photo: Scot Surbeck

This quilt illustrates how we stay in touch with others, across time and distance. The central column depicts travel across land, sea, and sky. The diagonal bands on either side suggest the evolving technology that we use to communicate when we are no longer in physical contact. Spools of thread are also included, because I feel that I remain forever connected to anyone to whom I have given a quilt. The border includes references to destinations around the world. A quilt with this theme has been in my mind for decades, as I started to collect the materials. Originally, I was thinking about the westward expansion of the United States, and the ways in which people maintained connections with family and friends when they were physically separated. Sometimes the connection included a quilt. I used to wonder what would be the impetus to finally start the quilt. In mid-March, the coronavirus pandemic forced a new type of separation. The act of touching has taken on new significance. We need to be in touch, but without touching. I decided that I should use the time that I would ordinarily be commuting to work in New York City to quilt. I decided that this was the right project for this special time. Working in quarantine, I feel the need to make decisions quickly and to keep focused. This project has helped my mental health a great deal, as it was something positive within my control, where I could see daily results.

—*Teresa Barkley*
Maplewood, New Jersey, USA

I was originally inspired to create this quilt as a testament to my musical communication with God. As the COVID-19 pandemic progressed and my friends died, and then I watched George Floyd being murdered, I realized that this quilt represented my communication to my fellow human beings as well. This is not a self-portrait but rather a testament to my obligation to say something! To let my voice be heard among the throngs of people who stand for justice.

—*Linda F. Martin*
Hartford, Connecticut, USA

Opposite: Geraldine Warner, *In Nature's Realm*, 56 × 48 in.

The struggles of the COVID-19 pandemic of 2020 are embedded in our memories forever. This highly contagious infection ravages lives—no matter the color, economic background, age, or gender of its victims. The subsequent quarantine and social shutdown of almost all of our daily activities have changed our realities. But there are people who are more vulnerable to being fatally harmed by such an odious illness, including those with underlying health issues. According to experts, African Americans are four times more likely to die from COVID due to socioeconomic disadvantages that have persisted for hundreds of years. Their suffering is disproportionate to that of white people. An added burden stems from loss of employment during the pandemic. Low wages strain and overly burden the African American spirit. On May 25, 2020, George Floyd was killed by police. Another young black man is murdered. Let's summarize these combustible facts. The fuels, if you will, are simply stated: COVID-19, unemployment, and continuous racial brutality spark the soul. The fire in the minds and souls of people who have endured so many hardships are finally ignited. Weeks of protests, mostly peaceful, some violent, by people of all races join in speaking out all over the world. The choice to die by police or COVID is at the forefront. Many people are no longer fearful but empowered in this moment to express themselves freely. Rallying calls, looting, violence, and fires begin the chain of events the day after Floyd's death.

—*Miki Rodriguez*
San Antonio, Texas, USA

"The only cure for loneliness, despair, and hopelessness is love."

—**Mother Teresa,** *A Simple Path*

Opposite: Teresa Barkley, *Stay in Touch*, 84 × 60 in.
Photo: Deidre Adams

Linda F. Martin, *I Will Life Up My Voice*, 39 × 30 in.

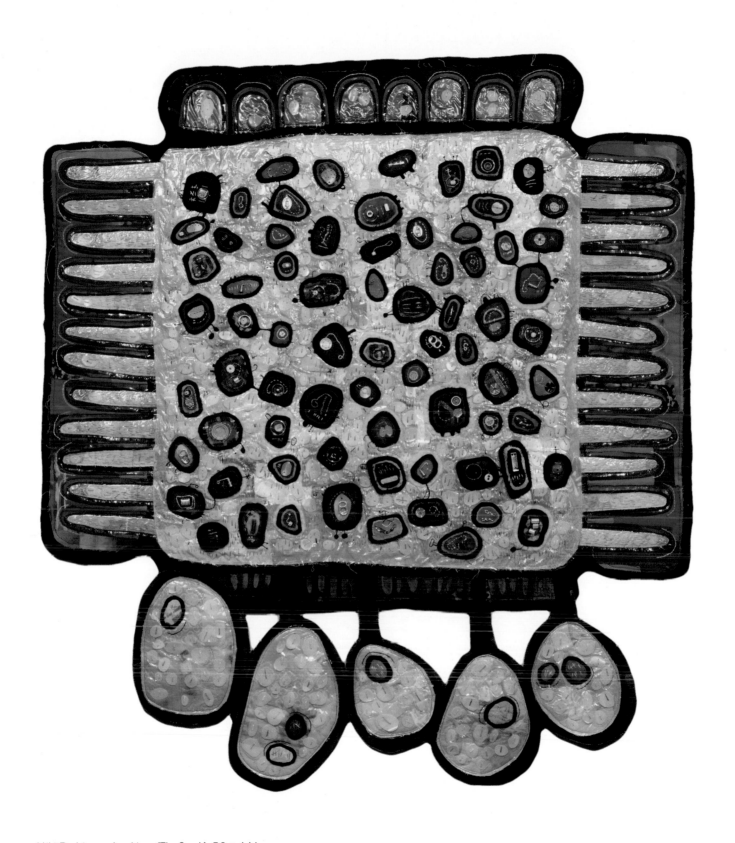

Miki Rodriguez, *La chispa (The Spark)*, 50 × 44 in.
Photo: Ansen Seale

Wisconsin Museum of Quilts and Fiber Arts: *The Quarantine Quilt*

In early March 2020, the Wisconsin Museum of Quilts and Fiber Arts in Cedarburg (WMQFA) launched a collaborative art project to give fiber artists a chance to stay home, stay safe, and keep creating. The Quarantine Quilt Community Art Project originated in the last few minutes of the staff's first virtual meeting during the COVID-19 outbreak and subsequent quarantines and "safer-at-home" orders in Wisconsin. Devyn McIlraith, the collections manager and education coordinator, proposed the idea for making a quarantine quilt with an open call for anyone affected by the quarantines to submit a quilt block that would become a documentation of this time in history. The project was swiftly approved and launched March 17 on the museum's social media pages. With a few minor adjustments, it was then submitted as a press release and picked up by local news sources. By mid-June 2020, the museum had received more than three hundred quilt blocks and the original post had been viewed more than sixty thousand times. Blocks were requested to be 12 by 12 inches, with a 1-inch seam allowance (leaving 1 inch of the 12-inch block plain on each edge).

WMQFA executive director Melissa Wraalstad stated on the museum's website: "We know everyone is facing uncertain and frightening times. But art has the unique power to bring us together. Even as we self-isolate and quarantine, this project reminds us that we are still a community, and we can create something beautiful to express ourselves." The project represents a community of fiber artists, a collective of individuals of all ages, who are experiencing a similar story in different places with fiber art as the unifying factor. Many of the blocks have included stories or words of wisdom or just notes of love and support from all over the country. The museum has even received a block from The Netherlands and from many parts of Wisconsin, as well as other states, including California, Florida, Illinois, New York, Missouri, and Washington.

Each block is unique and tells the story, through fiber art, of an individual experiencing quarantine. These blocks represent family, friends, love, community, support, inward or outward reflections on the situation, personal stories, new hobbies (some first-time quilt block makers) and well-seasoned expertise, joy, sadness, and a shared experience, all through the medium of fiber. The quilt blocks show an enormous diversity of techniques and processes. Some are embroidered and embellished blocks. Others are on recycled T-shirts, cross-stitched, pieced or appliquéd blocks, marker decorated, painted fabrics, collages with photos either attached or printed on, felt blocks, woven blocks, rug-hooked blocks, and various other fiber and textile bases.

The job of creating each finished quilt is enormous, but several of the museum's volunteers quickly stepped up and organized their completion. The quilts were displayed at the museum in an exhibition designed by WMQFA's Curator Emily Schlemowitz from August 7 through November 15, 2020. This exhibition is currently available to other institutions for touring.

More information and images of completed blocks can be found at https://www.wiquiltmuseum.com/the-quarantine-quilt.

Note: This text was supplied by the Museum. The digital image published here of a digital "quilt" formed by twelve of the squares is by the author.

Squares from *The Quarantine Quilt*
Left to right and top to bottom:
Row 1: Karen Pollard (Lake Mills, Wisconsin), Laura McCormack (Plainfield, Illinois), Nari Haig (Whitefish Bay, Wisconsin)
Row 2: Kathy DeVries (Milwaukee, Wisconsin), Robert Tucker (Rancho Mirage, California), Bonnie Connolly (Sturgeon Bay, Wisconsin)
Row 3: Hannah King (Buffalo, Minnesota), Kristy Carroll (Kearney, Missouri), Tink Linhart (Grafton, Wisconsin)
Row 4: Mary Mauer (Cedarburg, Wisconsin), Mary Zimmerman (Spring Green, Wisconsin), Pat Shaver (Lombard, Illinois)
Photos of individual quilt squares courtesy of the Wisconsin Museum of Quilts and Fiber Arts.

"To be alone—the eternal refrain of life. It wasn't better or worse than anything else."

—ERICH MARIA REMARQUE,
Arch of Triumph: A Novel of a Man without a Country

CHAPTER ONE

Coronavirus Circling the Globe

By now (September 2020), the spherical shape of COVID-19 particles with their club-shaped nodules must be familiar to most of the world. The protein nodules allow the particles to latch onto cells, making us sick. In this chapter, quilts featuring or suggesting the coronavirus sphere depict the nodules in various ways, including three-dimensionality. Their main model is an illustration created by the Centers for Disease Control and Prevention (CDC), where the sphere is grayish and the nodules are red and bulbous. Depending on how the particles are depicted in the quilts, they range from sinister to decorative, the latter approach perhaps being one way to deal with pervasive fear of COVID-19.

The final three quilts in this chapter reflect statistics relating to infection rates and death, with Juna Carle's chart inspired by an article in *the Washington Post* recording the "precarious nature of our times." As of late August, 844,000 people worldwide have died, including 64,000 in India; 121,000 in Brazil; and 183,000 in the United States. The US death toll is predicted by the CDC to reach more than 200,000 before the end of September, especially with COVID-19 apparently out of control in several states—such as Texas, where the *Quarantine Quilts* exhibition was canceled, and California, which grips me personally as my children and grandchildren live in Los Angeles and Oakland. It could be a very long time before I see them again, and I fear for their safety.

Artists' Narratives

This is a quilt I did for my daughter who is a data scientist for Biobot Analytics in Boston. The company tests sewage water to assess prevalence of COVID-19 in communities. I chose the background fabric to represent the 170 cities currently tested; the center is a sewer manhole with a histogram made of people and curves, and the red spikes are my interpretation of the virus.

—Nadine Pédusseau
San Diego, California, USA

I started this quilt the first week of quarantine, March 15, 2020, not dreaming that we would still be living a quarantine life so many months later. I tend to make art quilts that tell the stories of current events, so I had to make a COVID-19 piece. This quilt started with the COVID-like circle in the center. Then I started adding images and instructions in a kaleidoscopic sort of way to represent the virus spreading all over the world. I have to admit I was scared, nervous, and worried the whole time I was making this quilt. It felt like such chaos. Even though the instructions to stay safe were so simple, people were still not believing or following the guidelines, some for lack of leadership. I've watched a lot of news and slept more than I ever have during this time. I will continue to make quilts that speak of all that is happening and dream of life being "normal" again.

—Sylvia Hernandez
Brooklyn, New York, USA

The COVID virus knocked the world off its axis. It seemed that danger lurked everywhere and in every person you met. And we ourselves were a potential danger to others. Even simple, routine things like grocery shopping became life-threatening. And then it got scarier. Fed up with police violence, people took to the streets to protest for Black Lives Matter. Some wore masks for protection. Others didn't, and the virus reached even greater levels of infection. We were told that the safest place was home. So we stayed home. But what was once a haven from the world began to close in on us and became suffocating. The only safe way to connect with others was through electronic devices so we clung to that beacon of light in a world gone mad.

—Jayne Bentley Gaskins
Reston, Virginia, USA

Nadine Pédusseau, *Pandemic*, 28.5 × 29.5 in.

Sylvia Hernandez, *Corona 2020*, 44 × 44 in.

Jayne Bentley Gaskins, *The Light Within*, 34.5 × 34.5 in.

Susan Allen, *COVID-19*, 24 in. diameter

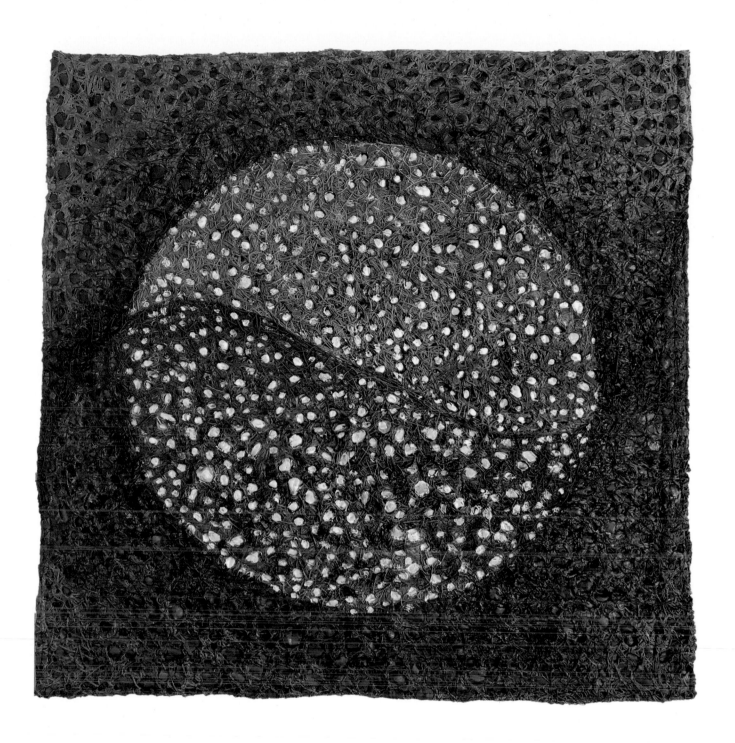

Shin-hee Chin, *Mysterious Grace*, 29 × 29 in.

During social distancing, feeling disconnected from the world, media inundations about COVID-19 created images and thoughts that needed expression. The national chaos needed to be expressed artistically in chaotic and random fabric pieces, as I did in my quilt.

—*Susan Allen*
West Linn, Oregon, USA

The pandemic has brought great stress and uncertainty into our everyday lives. Paradoxically, however, it also gives us a chance to reconnect to nature, realizing the significance of maintaining a harmonious lifestyle with our environment. In that sense, it could be a disguised blessing. This phenomenon of harmony is well reflected in the ancient Chinese philosophy of yin and yang. It is a concept of dualism: two halves that together complete wholeness by chasing after each other as they seek a new balance.

—*Shin-hee Chin*
Hillsboro, Kansas, USA

We entered 2020 with big dreams and hopes for the year. Then COVID spreads and we are caught in a cycle of despair and fear circled around a microscopic virus. My hope is we eventually recover, leave the coil, and never return.

—*Candice Murray*
Dalton, Georgia, USA

As I was sewing this pattern during quarantine, I kept seeing spores and strands. The song "My Sharona" from the 1970s popped into my head, but instead I was singing "My Corona," and the name has stuck.

—*Terri Lynn Normoyle*
Porter, Texas, USA

After a knee replacement followed by a five-week hospitalization in May 2018, a virus, not this 2020 coronavirus, left me unable to walk. My lifelong quilting passion was a healing journey. During the last seventy-eight days as I wheeled around my fabric stash, sewing machine, and tools—cutting and fusing—I seemed to be going in circles. Now, on May 18, I am celebrating *Dancing Circles*, on my eighty-sixth birthday. Still haven't gone full circle.

—*Jo Lee Tarbell*
Charlottesville, Virginia, USA

Candice Murray, *COVID Coil*, 26 × 26 in.

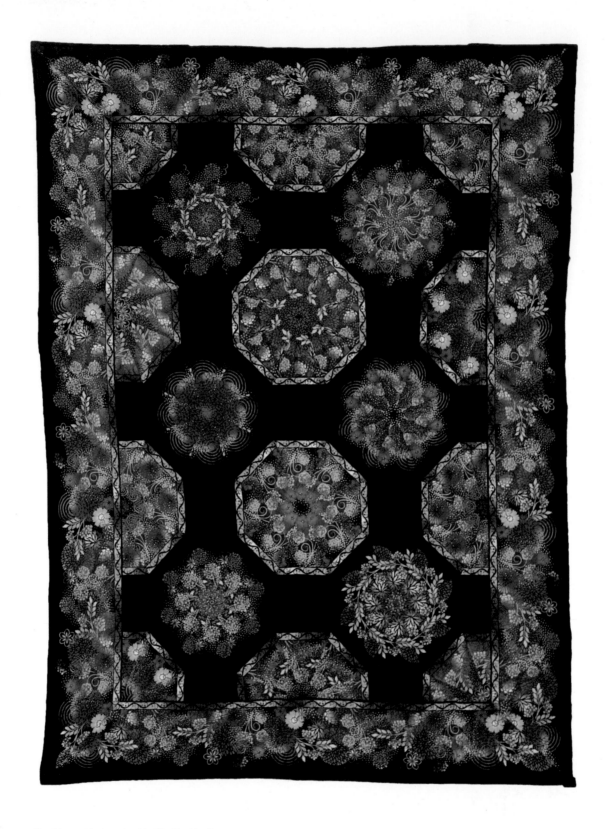

Terri Lynn Normoyle, *Ma Ma Ma My Corona*,
84 × 60 in.

OPPOSITE: Jo Lee Tarbell, *Dancing Circles, Staying in Line*, 80 × 60 in.

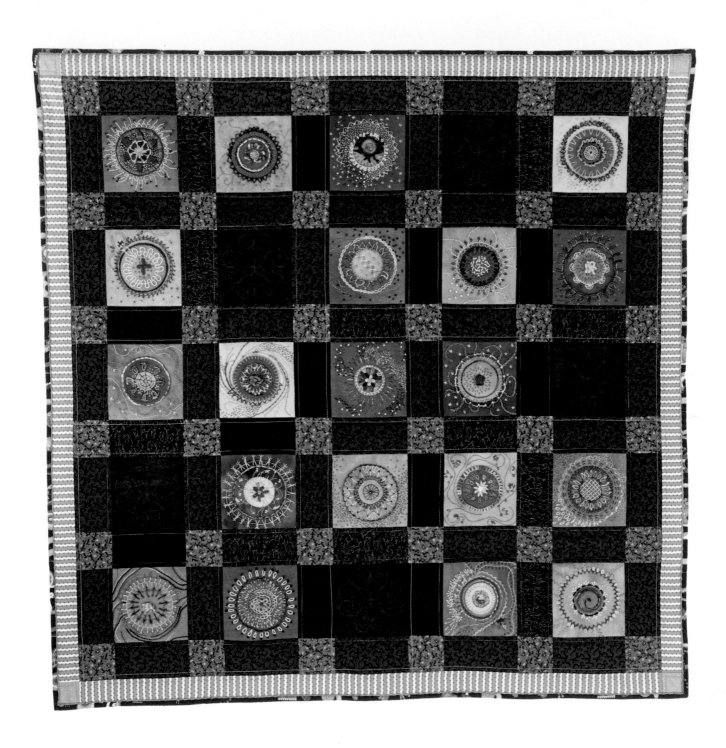

Margaret Ann Atwater Guldner, *New Jersey Beauties: My Corona*, 43 × 43 in.

Marlene Shea, *After the Storm—Flowers Will Bloom Again*, 24.5 × 25 in.

Biologically beautiful and complex, the science of viruses and SARS-CoV-2 informs and inspires these embellished varieties, reminiscent of illuminated manuscripts from medieval monasteries. I quarantined for several months in rural New Jersey, caring for my mother during her recuperation from surgery, while the virus mushroomed worldwide, proliferating nearby. Concern for my mother's health was paramount. If I left her house, I could return with the virus, so I stayed in. Any additional clarity found from sifting through the data and news stream proved elusive. I am normally levelheaded, purposeful, and organized, relishing time alone with long hours devoted to projects. But in this circumstance, I vacillated, flitted, and dithered, not because I was bored, just wholly distracted. Ultimately the routine of lists, small projects, and long walks reconstructed my focus. I had brought 5-inch wool squares which had malingered in my to-do pile for too long. My mother's new normal also came into focus. She was safe in her home. I needed to return to my home and husband who had endured alone, working from home, and watching his family suffer COVID-19 from afar. The five solid blocks of my quilt represent family members who contracted COVID-19.

—*Margaret Ann Atwater Guldner*
Houston, Texas, USA

Being confined to the house is very bad for me as an artist because my ideas are influenced by my surroundings. I live alone, and for the first month in isolation I just sat around thinking about the whole situation, not feeling very creative. Then I saw the *Quarantine Quilts* call for entries, and such competitions always excite me. I decided to see if I could change my state of mind and do something that would perk me up. I thought that there's always a light at the end of the tunnel and I would make this quilt to represent that. I started to get excited, looking for fabrics among my stash, as I couldn't go fabric shopping. I spotted the background fabric, which reminded me of the virus shape. So I was on my way, feeling confident in this noncreative period. Then a few days later, I became ill and was tested for COVID-19. During the three-day wait period for results, I was unproductive. When the results came back negative, I was relieved and ready to get back to my quilt. I was grateful I had this project to keep me interested and busy, and found I was liking the quilt more and more every day. It also made me feel like I was ready to start another challenge, which proved that there is light at the end of the tunnel.

—*Marlene Shea*
Wethersfield, Connecticut, USA

OPPOSITE: Whitney Dahlberg, *Untitled*, 11.5 × 6.5 in. (14 × 9 in. framed)

As I created this autobiographical work, my emotional turmoil played out on the cloth. These feelings were worked through in each stitch. As we faced the pandemic and isolated ourselves, this quilt, and the slow hand-stitching that went into it, took on a therapeutic and meditative response, allowing for a sense of calm.

—Whitney Dahlberg
Hagerstown, Maryland, USA

Michele Makinen, *The Coronavirus Web*, 46.5 × 58 in.
Photo: Monika Wulfers

Juna Carle, *Flatten the Curve*, 34 × 30 in.

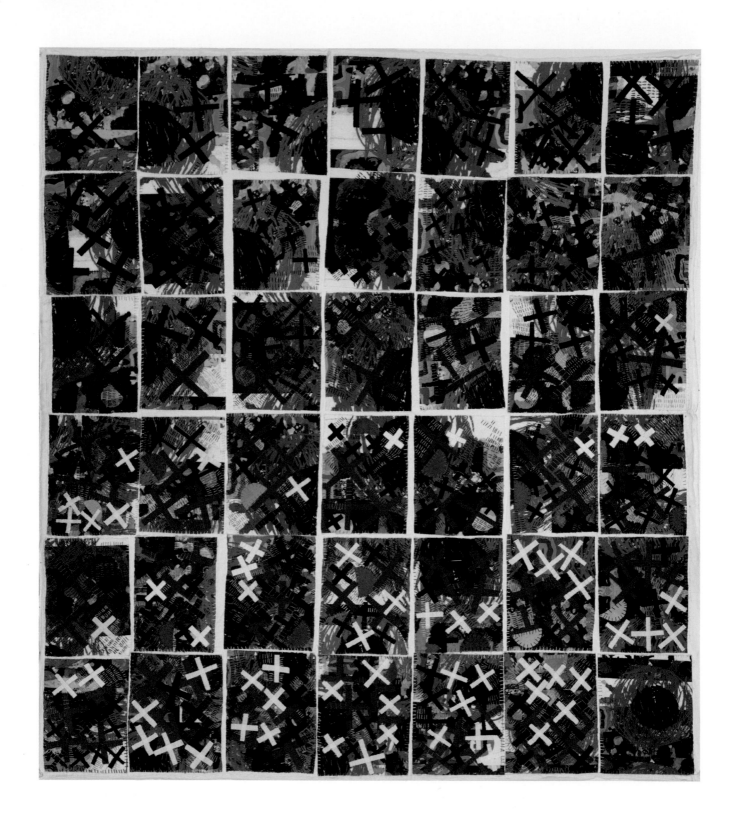

Susie Monday, *7 Days, 6 Weeks*, 58 × 53.5 in.
Photo: Ansen Seale

In March 2020, when lockdowns seemed inevitable, we moved from our condo in Chicago to a house in a small community an hour away. It felt like we were fleeing the apocalypse and I was filled with tension, but outwardly pretty calm. A few days before we left, I abandoned a new quilting project, as I couldn't focus, and worked on a quilt from a book, as that was distracting and soothing. I took with me fabric for masks and more quilting supplies plus unfinished quilts. When I would sew masks, my back hurt—I complained that it was my chair but it was anxiety for sure. I made many masks for friends and family, and also for those in an assisted-living facility near our home in Chicago. The Wisconsin Museum of Quilts and Fiber Arts requested blocks for a quarantine quilt, and I used playful fabrics and designs, which helped to cheer me up. Members of my Chicago quilting guild were very supportive.

As I steeped myself in sad statistics regarding the pandemic, thoughts began to form of how I would make a quilt representing the crisis. One of my first thoughts was to use a base of one hundred people and to represent them using all different fabrics, as everyone is unique. I represented those who died using a lace-patterned plastic, which made them somewhat invisible, as I thought that showed reverence. Then I added orange netting to give the feeling of people being trapped by the virus infections, and statistics for context.

—Michele Makinen
Chicago, Illinois, USA

In each section, the orange curve represents people infected over time. The lavender represents people who recovered, while neutral gray is for those never affected. Dark brown represents those who did not survive. We still don't know the total numbers. I like how the tipping nature of the rows expressed the precarious nature of our times. It was quilted to look like graph paper. (Inspired by an article in the *Washington Post* by Harry Stevens on March 14, 2020.)

—Juna Carle
Sonoma, California, USA

When Bexar County, Texas (the nearest metropolitan area), announced its first COVID-19 death on March 22, and quarantine was in the news, I decided to make a piece of art that would help me make the numbers real. This quilt, with its black Xs for deaths, individual stitches for confirmed cases, and white Xs for tens of those who recovered, is the result.

—Susie Monday
Pipe Creek, Texas, USA

"That polar privacy A soul admitted to itself— Finite infinity."

—EMILY DICKINSON,
"There Is a Solitude of Space"

CHAPTER TWO

Home Is Where the Art Is

Our homes should be our sanctuaries, even if life partners can be cranky, babies cry through the night, and teenagers sulk in their rooms. But during quarantine, home can become a prison precisely because it is our safe place, especially for those hunkered down in small apartments in high-rise buildings. To my mind, that situation seems like living in a vertical cruise ship, with its accompanying perils of infection and threat of monotony, one of our worst mental enemies during lockdown.

As several of the makers in this book have mentioned, most serious quilters were prepared for quarantine—and, in fact, have been for their entire adult lives. Except for those who work in surface design processes, which often require print shops and similar nonresidential spaces, quilt makers collect fabrics (their "stash") and other supplies, usually not knowing exactly what might be needed for a specific project.

The originality of quilts in this chapter reveals the ingenuity of several artistic minds being inspired by materials and subjects that, prequarantine, might not have resulted in quilts. Who would expect a quilt constructed from actual toilet-paper tubes or from the square cardboard pieces of vacuum-cleaner filter bags? Here we also have Susan Lenz's actualization of a solitary, isolated figure marking off the days until she loses count, and Brooke Atherton's quarantine tent combining both home and art, recalling the pandemic field hospitals in several of our cities.

Artists' Narratives

A "refugium" is an area where a population of organisms can survive through a period of unfavorable conditions. My family used this tent; the canvas drew a circle of protection around us in the night. It's filled with happy memories and laughter. *Refugium* is one of three works begun early in 2020 as a response to COVID-19. All are constructed from familiar things already part of my life. One is a timeline of the days spent sheltering at home, another is a warning about our reactions to events. The third is the tent. To help restore a sense of order, I assigned myself the task of hand-stitching two Log Cabin quilt blocks each evening. The first ones were made from tea bags saved by friends; as time passed, I switched to yellow and blue cotton blocks. A few were made by a friend who gave them to me, and she included fabric cut into strips. All I had to do was sew them together. Eventually, the traditional variations stopped holding my focus, and my mind started wandering to questions such as "What did Penelope think about while she wove, waiting for Ulysses to return?" While I waited for "normal" to return, I started making Frank Lloyd Wright–inspired Log Cabins, a twist to amuse myself.

—*Brooke Atherton*
Billings, Montana, USA

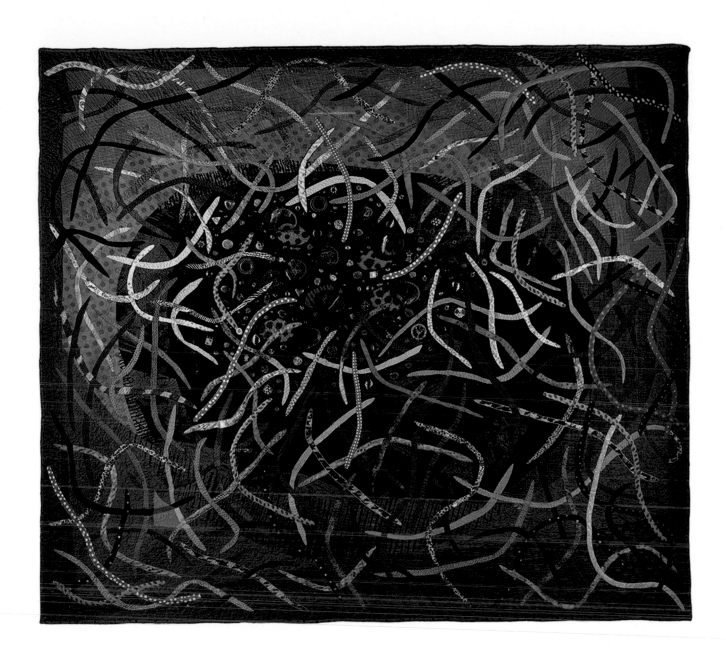

OPPOSITE: Brooke Atherton, *Refugium*, 141 × 206 in.
Photo: Dixie Yelvington

Terrie Hancock Mangat, *Crow's Nest*, 69 × 77 × 0.5 in.
Photo: Barry Norris

Crow's Nest was made deep into the quarantine time as I thought about nests and nesting. After my piece was machine quilted by Nicole Dunn, I hand-sewed on a stash of shiny objects that a crow or raven might find in New Mexico. It also has big egg shapes of mica I bought from a vendor hawking gemstones out by the Rio Grande Gorge Bridge (before quarantine). I love putting on the mica in the traditional Indian shisha technique of sewing on small reflective pieces. I have been so isolated! I love this story: my photographer, Barry Norris, told me about his mother sewing in spite of her terrible affliction of polio when she was thirty-four, weeks before the vaccine got to Germany where they were living.

—*Terrie Hancock Mangat*
El Prado, New Mexico, USA

Shelter in Place features vintage blocks, clothing, and fragments. The home is at the heart, but the sadness of our pandemic surrounds our sanctuary. The outer blocks are the Hands All Around pattern, representing how we must all come together to support and uplift each other. The bright star blocks suggest hope. The black fabrics are mourning prints from the 1880s that reflect the loss we have experienced as a nation.

—*Mary Wilson Kerr*
Woodbridge, Virginia, USA

Confession: I find quarantine too comfortable. I enjoy working at home, marooned with my family. So, it's not my mind I'm losing, but I feel I may be losing some heart. Who is my neighbor? Why should I care? Separated but not separate, we are all connected.

—*Amy Krasnansky*
Baltimore, Maryland, USA

Mary Wilson Kerr, *Shelter in Place*, 30 × 30 in.

My quilt was inspired by an Exuberant Appliqué class with Alethea Ballard. Here are what some of the images mean to me.

Middle left: These images represent the ways I can reach out to my friends. The world represents the internet, social media, and Zoom meetings accessed through my computer. Public television provides a window onto the world while staying home. My phone has become a lifeline to keep connected. My cat provides comfort, as he reminds me to enjoy the present. Since I am in the high-risk group due to health issues, I take many naps, and I must stay home to avoid contagion.

Amy Krasnansky, *Keep the Home Fires Burning*, 26 × 34 in.

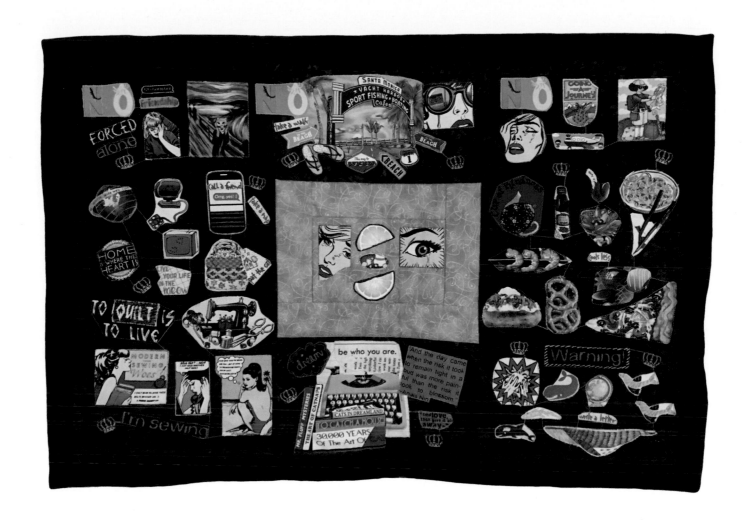

Middle right: These are the foods that I've been eating during the quarantine. I've had cup after cup of hot tea, reminding myself to drink slowly and relax. The bottle of soy sauce, bowl of vegetables, and dish of ramen noodles show my love of Asian food. The fortune cookie label shows "Today is yours," because today is the only day we have. I'm not a cook, so I have ordered food delivery many times during the lockdown. My favorite foods include shrimp, potatoes, pretzels, and pizza. There's also a strawberry covered in chocolate, as well as several chocolate goodies.

—*Betsy Barker*
Los Angeles, California, USA

Betsy Barker, *Corona Virus Blues*, 23 × 33 in.

Everything usual changed abruptly. Amidst uncertainty, colleges closed, classes went online, and so did graduations. This quilt is a celebration of graduations—my daughter's from Parsons and my son's from Clarkson. This is to say, from the isolation of quarantine, that I celebrate you and your achievements and wish you a future where whatever you wish to be, will be.

—*Jovita Revathi Vas*
Columbia, Maryland, USA

The ongoing quarantine due to COVID-19 as well as the seemingly increasing chaos in the world has inspired me to think more deeply and to develop a more peaceful vision for our planet as expressed by my art quilt *All of Us Together*: earth, animals, plants, and humans, old and new, in every color, shape, size, regardless of appearance, are all interconnected with a common denominator of love and forgiveness. The central motif of my quilt is a reproduction of *Animal Spiral*, a quilt I made in 1989. The surrounding faces are cloth versions of a recent series of drawings called "Faces of Equality, A–Z." The larger animal images forming the outer border of this artwork are derived from drawings by Ian May, Ethan Marks, and myself, all of us at home together.

—*Therese May*
San Jose, California, USA

With my travel schedule, it was always hard for me to find studio time. However, COVID caused all of my quilt history lectures and workshops to be canceled for months. I had never done a quilt for kids before and decided to explore this option based on eighteenth-century palampores made in India. I hand-painted the center medallion, which was then digitally printed on fabric. I wanted this quilt to be fun for kids, but also wanted kids to be able to learn from it. In the center of each border block is a surprise with some hand-painted details. The top row is the sun, moon, and stars. Bugs, bees, and butterflies fly down the sides. The row across the bottom is full of animals. Artistic, educational, and functional—what more could you want?

—*Lori Lee Triplett*
Overland Park, Kansas, USA

Jovita Revathi Vas, *An Unusual Celebration*, 34 × 34 in.

Therese May, *All of Us Together*, 84 × 96 in.

Lori Lee Triplett, *"Find It" Kids' Quilt*, 33 × 29 in.

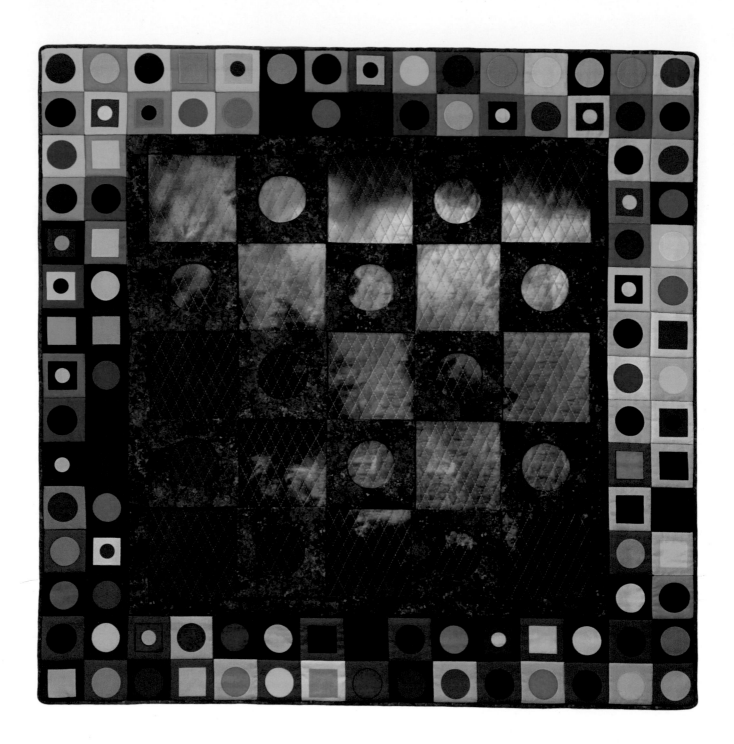

Jackie Gaskins, *Filtered*, 28.5 × 28.5 in.

Linda Kim, *T.P. Mania*, 38 × 38 in.

I made several masks using vacuum-cleaner bags as filters. These bags use a cardboard square with a round hole to attach to the vacuum cleaner. The shape of these perfectly cut squares inspired my quilt design. The actual vacuum-cleaner squares are now encapsulated in the quilt. These twelve squares were individually joined to form a see-through overlay, and represent the filters in the forty-eight masks that were made. Weekly Zooming with two of my four quilting bees feels like visits to everyone's studio without the one-hour commute. I love being able to share our projects and getting everyone's feedback. Since most of my family lives outside of the United States, I am accustomed to infrequent contact and the isolation has not really affected me. Quite the opposite! Since I recently bought a smartphone and discovered Facetime and Zoom, I have been strengthening family ties and reviving old friendships. I have seen the inside of my siblings' homes and had tours of their gardens. And I met my great-grandchildren.

—*Jackie Gaskins*
Virginia Beach, Virginia, USA

The humble toilet paper made headline news for weeks. As fear and frenzy gripped people around the world, I've tried to reflect this shared and surreal experience.

—*Linda M. Kim*
Austin, Texas, USA

Being stuck in my studio all day, every day, was like a dream come true, especially during a beautiful springtime in South Carolina. In many respects, quarantine was so fabulous that it was difficult to comprehend the dire straits in overcrowded hospitals, the need for masks, and the panic over too few ventilators. But that's what happened. Just because I wasn't going stir-crazy didn't mean others weren't counting the hours, days, and weeks. Thinking about other people made a difference. My imagination saw a lonesome guy marooned on a deserted island using a sharpened rock on a cliff wall to mark the passing time. One stroke upright, two, three, four, and a diagonal slash for every five days. It would be easy to stitch, a simple and universal illustration, just like prisoners awaiting their release. The phrase "stir-crazy" already suggested a crazy quilt. It was fun stitching a functional quilt top, but it was so much more fun to hand-stitch all the little counting lines. I have no idea how many there are. I got lost in the process, probably went a little stir-crazy myself.

—*Susan Lenz*
Columbia, South Carolina, USA

OPPOSITE: Susan Lenz, *Stir-Crazy in South Carolina*,
32.5 × 24.5 in.

I miss my friends; I miss my daily walks in the state park. I miss going out for sushi. There are so many things that I miss due to COVID-19. I Zoom with my friends and family and we get takeout now for sushi. There is a gaping hole in my heart. The hug that used to put a Band-Aid on that little bruise on my heart is gone. The little fish on my shoulder is telling me, "It's gonna be okay." I miss what I took for granted.

—*Trish Morris-Plise*
Nevada City, California, USA

My quilt *Dancing with My Heart in the Garden of Life* was created for the 2020 Quilt Challenge of a March Madness Shop Hop. The theme was "Garden Party." This shop hop was March 12–14, 2020. It was odd driving around in the Bay Area, as there was very little traffic that weekend. This was the last major outing I went on just before the shelter-in-place mandate. During the COVID quarantine, I busied myself creating flowers, leaves, and vines. What I thought would take a few hours multiplied into weeks. I was grateful for the quarantine period so that I could focus on getting it done. Much of the hand sewing occurred during Zoom meetings. Working on this quilt has brought a joy to my spirit, as it represents my life. I have been very sick for the last ten years. I feel like God is awakening my heart to life again. As my heart is awakening, my life is blooming with love and the fragrance of joy. The butterflies represent freedom from pain and suffering. The background represents the light as it dispels the darkness, bringing hope, truth, and a future filled with blessings.

—*Shelley Worsham*
Oakdale, California, USA

"I am so utterly lonely, but I also have such a fear that my isolation be broken through, and I no longer be the head and ruler of my universe."

—**Anaïs Nin,**
House of Incest

OPPOSITE: Trish Morris-Plise, *The Year That Left a Hole in My Heart*, 40.5 × 27 in.

Shelley Worsham, *Dancing with My Heart in the Garden of Life*,
41 × 43 in. Quilted by Tracey Boss.

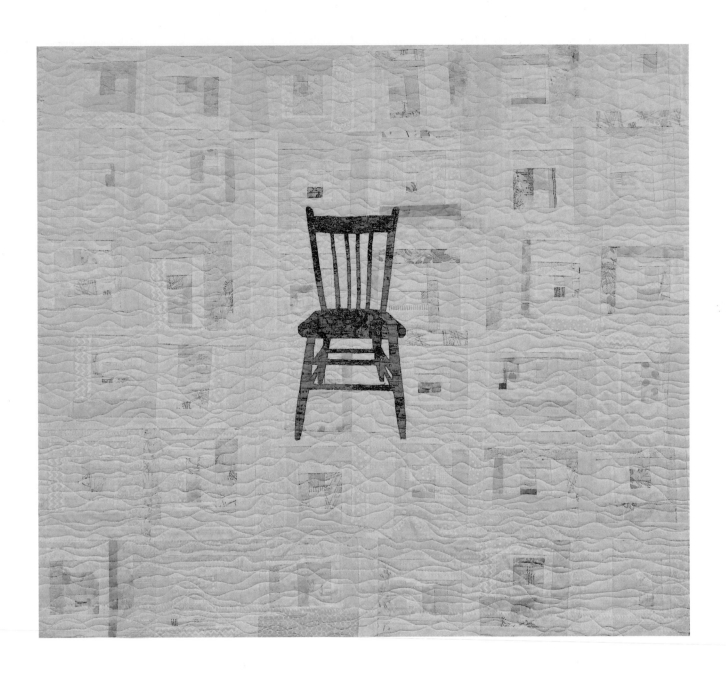

Maggie Vanderweit, *Sitting & Waiting*, 50 × 56 in.

In a series of work called Room at the Table I have been using this simple antique chair image to symbolize belonging and inclusion. The chair in this piece is lonelier than my others. The world has quieted, we are isolated and uncertain, and our lives have been disrupted by the COVID-19 pandemic in previously unimaginable ways. The simple white wonky Log Cabin background, quilted in irregular waves, is for the new face of our weirdly empty new world, and the waves and winds of change. The chair is made from map fabric and it is blown slightly askew. However, it is steadily holding the place where we wait patiently and try our best to maintain hope. We sit and imagine life as it will be, different but OK. We sit and believe that everything will work out, even though we don't know how.

—*Maggie Vanderweit*
Fergus, Ontario, Canada

Home is often described as a safe haven, but it may not feel safe for those dealing with depression, loneliness, or abuse. As a retired teacher, I have witnessed or experienced these problems firsthand. Even though I personally feel safe at home, I could imagine, as did many others, an unnerving sense of imprisonment when the shelter-in-place order came to our locale in March. Like many quilters, I immersed myself in sewing. I was grateful to have enough fabrics on hand to pull out a cloud novelty fabric in my stash, pairing it with a depiction of a small cottage printed as a watercolor on fabric by a West Coast artist, Judith M. Kirby. The home placed in the clouds represented a beautiful abode floating in a surreal world; we were no longer grounded, because the world outside was unsafe.

—*Linda Mazunik*
Lone Tree, Colorado, USA

Linda Mazunik, *Safer at Home*, 30 × 30 in.

"If we winter this one out, we can summer anywhere."

—SEAMUS HEANEY
(1972 interview)

CHAPTER THREE

Be Smart, Be Vigilant

Three of the international artists fall within this chapter, from COVID hot spots in Australia and Spain, addressing the subjects of isolation and masks. While Inmaculada Gabaldon was inspired by a carnival mask in Venice, her quilt delves into what might be hidden behind a mask. I was fascinated by the bubbles in her quilt, wondering if they carried the virus as they captured the breath and floated it away. For me, "social distancing" of 3 feet or even 6 feet is not sufficient. Like multitudes of us living in fear across the globe, I have watched those YouTube videos of experiments suggesting that viral particles can travel 12 feet or more, expelled by a cough, sneeze, or even a laugh. In July, when infectious disease experts announced that the virus was airborne, I stopped worrying about how many feet of distance kept me safe and focused more on spending as little time as possible in the few places where I had to enter. I nagged my husband mercilessly when he wanted to browse in the grocery store: "Our fifteen minutes are up. Let's go!"

As in other chapters of the book, these artists proved their ingenuity in working with whatever materials were at hand. Quilt makers are famous for saving their remnants and scraps of fabric (let's not say "hoarding," such a mean word), a habit that served many of them well during times of quarantine. In addition, fabric remnants allowed quilters to make face masks for friends, family, hospital workers, cashiers in grocery stores, postal workers, and—my personal heroes out in rural Pennsylvania—the FedEx and UPS drivers. To be totally efficient, they then stitched scraps from their mask-making into some of the quilts in this book.

Artists' Narratives

The eagle waits and watches as the pandemic spreads over the world, knowing that soon he will fly again. As a textile sculptor, I enjoy molding fabric into 3-D birds, then layering more fabric for texture, and adding trim and other embellishments to create character.

—*Linda Fjeldsted Blust*
Reno, Nevada, USA

I made this quilt during the month of May 2020, in full confinement. Since I was unable to leave the house, I had to use fabric scraps from other jobs and as background a sheet from my mother's trousseau. This work has helped me to endure the difficult days that we have had during this tragic pandemic. The meaning of the quilt title, *Las apariencias engañan (Looks Are Deceiving)*, comes from the fact that the protagonist is not a woman, but a man in disguise (one of the many beautiful masks of the 2020 Venice Carnival), who served me as inspiration for my quilt.

—*Inmaculada Gabaldon*
Madrid, Spain

This work is a representation of my truncated view of the outside world during two weeks of mandatory isolation required for all Australians returning from overseas when COVID struck. My husband and I were partway through a holiday in Bolivia in mid-March, but we had to return quickly to Australia due to the growing global impact of COVID. We were relieved to be able to rebook our flights and even more relieved to step onto the final flight to Sydney. During our quarantine, we were dependent on the kindness of friends, and used online deliveries to buy groceries and provisions. Our bags of goods were left on our front step by the delivery person, who would talk to us from a distance through our screen door. This was my only face-to-face contact with anyone other than my husband during this time. I could use only materials I had on hand to make this piece. The background colors are waste thread from past projects. The black fabric for the silhouette and the white tulle were in my stash. To secure all the layers together, I stitched the grid pattern of my screen door in charcoal thread. This work will always remind me of the strange time during isolation and the feeling of being separate from the rest of the world.

—*Penny Howard*
Umina Beach, New South Wales, Australia

OPPOSITE: Linda Fjeldsted Blust, *Tomorrow I Soar*, 23.5 × 10.5 × 19 in.

Inmaculada Gabaldon, *Las apariencias engañan (Looks Are Deceiving)*, 35 × 46 in.

OPPOSITE: Penny Howard, *My COVID Days*, 10 × 4.5 in.
Photo: Stephen Cummings

Marjorie Madsen, *QUILTED 19—Quarantseam*, 29.5 × 29.5 in.

Crazy times call for crazy quilts! As an artist and quilter, the first thing I did was to make sure that friends and family were safe. I packed up my daughter from her college dorm in California, hit the road, stopped at Wi-Fi locations so she could Zoom to classes, and landed at home. Then I made masks. Lots of them, mailed and delivered to my favorite bacon-green-chili burrito shop, sewing-challenged friends and family throughout the US, and my auto repair shop people, who loved the pony and princess fabric from my stash. After New Mexico announced its lockdown on March 23, I hunkered down per the governor's decree, checked on friends, and monitored the news. The call for artists for this book inspired me, as I had just rediscovered a bag of men's tie remnants as well as several old silk blouses. I had been saving them to create a crazy quilt at some point in time—no time like the quarantine present. Recycled workwear seemed especially appropriate, given that these were no longer necessary for people working from home. Forty pieces for the quilt base seemed appropriate, as the book of Genesis states it rained forty days and nights during Noah's voyage, and the word "quarantine" derives from the Italian for forty days, *quaranta giorni*. Lastly, I designed hand-embroidery stitches inspired by nineteen major COVID-19 themes, and here are some of them: the virus itself, toilet paper, hand sanitizer, masks, medical crises, and . . . Corona beer!

—Marjorie Madsen
Los Alamos, New Mexico, USA

Blocks that I think of as petri dishes illustrate each person's experience during pandemic-mandated separation. Chain-link-fence bias tape adds another layer keeping us out (or in) and away from each other. A ghost block represents the blocks on the back from overseas delayed mail arrival. The quilt-making community will always overcome and make together even when we must be physically apart.

—Laura Loewen
Lafayette, Colorado, USA

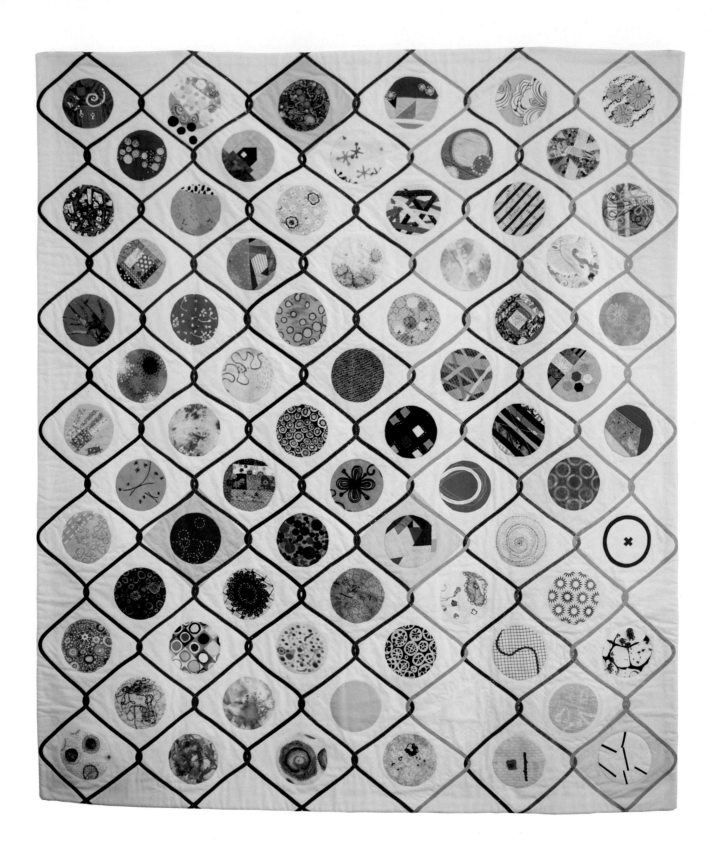

OPPOSITE: Laura Loewen, *Social Distancing Quilt*, 58 × 50 in.

Anna Tufankjian, *Smile with Your Eyes*, 24 × 24 in.

Suddenly I was living alone during a quarantine; mask wearing was becoming commonplace; and social distancing was here to stay. My calendar had been filled with social gatherings, lectures, performances, gallery openings, and now all were being Xed out. This was the new normal. I had been sharing my home with my sister, my muse of sorts, and tragically she passed away the very same week when it all began. Processing all these challenges was particularly difficult without any close human connection. Face masks covered the smiles and social distancing prevented the hugs. Making art quilts was always my choice of expressing myself. For over three weeks I couldn't think outside the box, couldn't come up with a way of showing how I felt or what I was missing most. I couldn't think outside the box because I was IN THE BOX. My box no longer had groups of artists with show and tell, bouncing ideas and options around, no gallery visits talking about our reactions to the works. I threw myself into sewing masks for days on end. In the midst of cutting my last scraps of elastic, the idea came to me that my art piece would be about what masks are doing to our feelings. My title is *Smile with Your Eyes*. We all need to give and get smiles, especially now. This process of creating my message occupied my mind and my heart, deflated my depression, and I was smiling again.

—Anna Tufankjian
Newington, Connecticut, USA

Today, we are making masks to fill the massive deficit of pandemic supplies that the government neglected to prepare because it was focused on letting corporations increase their profits. My quilt is intended to evoke backyard plots and the backing is made of remnants from sewing masks.

—Rebecca Cynamon-Murphy
Wheaton, Illinois, USA

My working life came to a halt when the pandemic struck. Everything I had planned for 2020 disappeared overnight and I was left with a void I had no idea how to fill. Fortunately, as an artist I could also turn to my art and so my studio became my refuge. Opportunities to create and also connect with other artists appeared, and although my life has changed, my future looks full of opportunities. Different ones but still exciting. While many doors have closed, ones I never expected or even knew about have opened. I'm thinking positively about the future.

—Lisa Walton
Lewisham, New South Wales, Australia

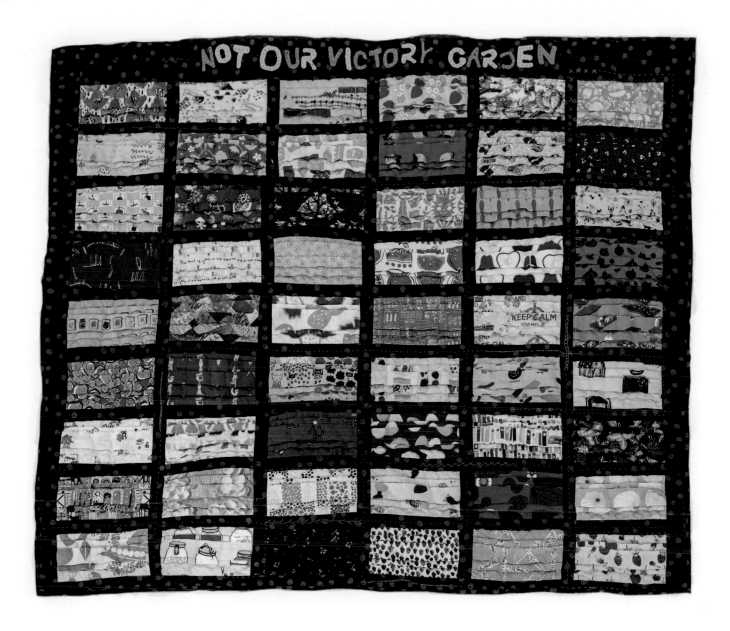

This quilt began with an improv-piecing challenge from my guild. I assembled the improvisational sections into an enclosed shape representing our efforts to contain the virus by mostly staying at home. The red channels represent how our half-hearted attempts have been insufficient.

—*Vasudha Govindan*
Houston, Texas, USA

Rebecca Cynamon-Murphy. *Not Our Victory Garden*, 45 × 40 in.
Photo: Erin Dobosiewicz

Lisa Walton, *Masks*, 40 × 28 in.

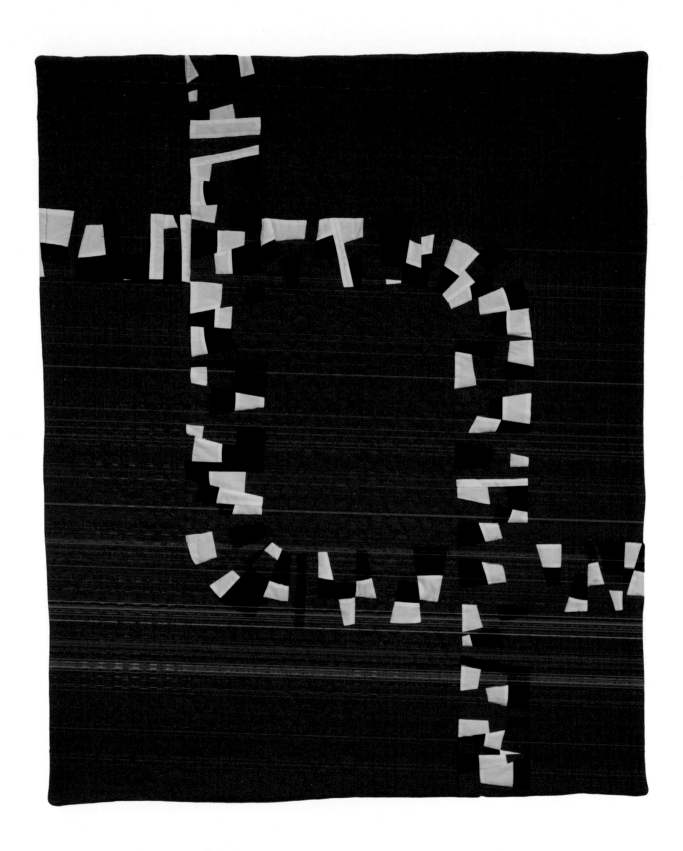

Vasudha Govindan, *Containment*, 41 × 35 in.

"I am not alone if I stand by myself."

—HENRY DAVID THOREAU,
A Week on the Concord and Merrimack Rivers

CHAPTER FOUR

Pandemic Patterns

Several of the makers in this book have mentioned that quarantine gave them the freedom to follow their own design instincts, while they had to manage with restricted access to materials and tools. One result is what we might call "mutated patterns," as in the quilts by Pat Forster, Shawn Geist, Lynn Hanna, and Kelly Spell. Other graphically abstract works contain shifts of color and sparks of light symbolizing hope for the future, including Kate Stiassni's *There Is Light at the End of the Tunnel*. Like many of the quilts in this book, the serendipity of whatever fabrics were on hand encouraged originality, even within templated patterns, such as Corinne Pitcher's interpretation of a design by Victoria Findlay Wolfe.

A world off-kilter informed the quilts by Pam Calderwood and Sharon Casey. As public health, the economy, and racial equality ran off the rails in this country, disjointed and unbalanced imagery worked its way not only into the examples selected for *Quarantine Quilts*, but also into dozens of works not included in the book. I wish that we could have published many more.

This chapter includes four of the international artists, from Australia, Switzerland, Great Britain at the height of contagion, and Venice as a cloud of death seemed to loom over the city. Giovanna Nicolai's *Mood Swings* represents the distraught emotions of Italy amid its staggering body count due to COVID-19, more than 35,000 as of August, and more than 2,000 in Venice alone.

Artists' Narratives

Under Siege began as a way to get out of the headspace I was in during the beginning of the lockdowns. I, like many people, was struggling. There has been quite a bit to deal with over these months, and in an effort to sort of escape within my home, I turned to art. In this case it was in the form of quilt design, so I grabbed my graph paper and pencils and got to it. As a distraction it worked—for me, there is nothing like putting on some inspiring music and drawing.

As a starting point for most of my designs in the summer of 2020, I've chosen to incorporate a triangle-in-a-square block. It was fun to draw blocks and then play with color placement. *Under Siege* is one of two wall hangings I made from stash fabric. Once I was able to go back to work quilting at a local shop, it was the first project I tackled to get back into the swing of things and was excited to submit it for consideration. My hope is that my quilt inspires other people to have fun with quilt design!

—*Amanda Bauer*
Aurora, Colorado, USA

I started this quilt before the COVID pandemic. During the first couple weeks of the pandemic, I was having a difficult time processing all the news. *Block Print 2*, a companion to another Block Print quilt, kept me busy and distracted from the never-ending news coverage.

—*Pam Calderwood*
Burlington, Iowa, USA

Fear and sadness gripped me when the United States first began learning about the coronavirus. The uncertainty surrounding the virus was omnipresent. Could I hug my grandchildren, speak to my friends while sitting in our backyard, or touch the fruits and vegetables at the grocery store? Making fiber art is my calming salve. I pulled out fabrics, cut individual hexagons, and English-paper-pieced them, each pull of the needle and thread helping to calm the fear and sadness. Using a piece of hand-dyed indigo my friend Jo Matthias made for me, I started placing the hexagons on the calm blue sea. Moving the hexagons into a pleasing pattern, I realized I was making pathways to a place unknown. Between the hexagon paths I found secret stars, a reminder that even in the midst of chaos there is good. Creating different pathways in the side borders, as well as the diagonal quilting, reinforced my understanding that there are many ways to get to a safe place—a state of mind as well as a journey.

—*Geneva Carroll*
West Richland, Washington, USA

Amanda Bauer, *Under Siege*, 42.5 × 42.5 in.

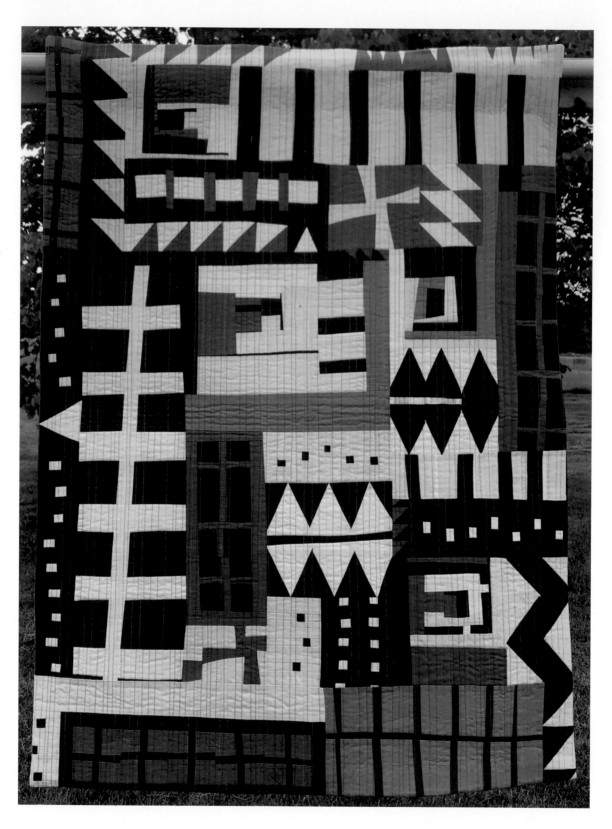

Pam Calderwood, *Block Print 2*, 46 × 33 in.

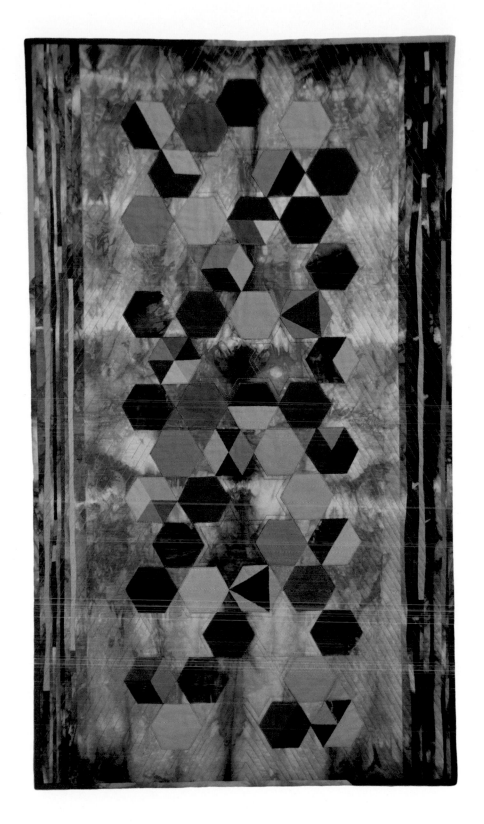

Geneva Carroll, *Pathways*, 42 × 23 in.
Photo: Robert L. Carroll

I love the natural beauty of rock cairns, with stones carefully balanced on top of one another. This is not one of those. The feeling in our country was becoming uncertain, and even chaotic, when I began this piece, and that was even before the coronavirus pandemic arrived here. With each news report, the tipping of the "stones" became more exaggerated as this double-sided cairn continued to grow upward. Day by day, it became more off-balance and topsy-turvy. It was as if the events swirling around us were manifesting in front of me.

—*Sharon Casey*
Bakersfield, California, USA

During the pandemic I have found safety inside, but remain focused on the seismic shifts in the world outside. *There Is Light at the End of the Tunnel* expresses both my imaginings and my desire to see into what the future might hold. During this unusual time, I am finding new joy in a smaller place and in what I can make with my own two hands.

—*Kate Stiassni*
Salisbury, Connecticut, USA

Quarantine for me brought a freedom to make without striving to meet exhibition standards. A call from our guild for single-bed quilts for teenagers, for the community quilt program, prompted me to choose vibrant colors. Then, I had fun drawing different configurations of Log Cabin blocks on grid paper, inspired initially by Carrie Strine's *Steps* quilt in *Simply Moderne*. This quilt was fun and quick to make, and a great distraction from COVID concerns. An added bonus was that my husband and son, who were in the house at the time, kept checking on the progress and really liked the result.

—*Pat Forster*
Mount Pleasant, Western Australia, Australia

OPPOSITE: Sharon Casey, *Precarious Times*, 72 × 58 in.

Kate Stiassni, *There Is Light at the End of the Tunnel*, 54 × 30 in.
Photo: Ren Nickson Photography

OPPOSITE: Pat Forster, *Crazy Quilt for a Crazy Time*, 72 × 54 in.

Shawn Geist, *Rocky Mountain Sunrise*, 71 × 52 in.

I work as a mail carrier and was deemed mission critical. No sheltering at home for me. Weekends in my quilt studio brought solitude from the chaos. Creating this quilt brought peace and calm to my mind. The sun continues to rise in my corner of the Rocky Mountains.

—*Shawn Geist*
La Junta, Colorado, USA

Our lives were moving along in regular rhythms and patterns until the COVID-19 quarantine orders. Suddenly our world took a giant wrong turn as fear of the virus infiltrated our thoughts and actions. Moving forward from here, lifestyles will be forever changed.

—*Lynn Hanna*
Loma Linda, California, USA

Going up and down and round and round the house and garden—that is what I do a lot while shielding at home. Keeping away from the deadly virus that lurks invisibly outside. My health issues mean I'm going to stay at home for quite a long time. I anxiously follow the developments in the search for a vaccine. During quarantine, having a reasonably sized house and garden is a luxury we must fully appreciate. The people in my street are kind to each other. We used to come out every Thursday evening to clap for our wonderful National Health Service and the hardworking staff that are out there in the frontline saving lives. Church bells rang for the doctors, nurses, and hospital staff of all levels. We were already aware of the importance of highly trained people for our health, but we also started to realize how crucial those in "low skilled," badly paid jobs, like cleaning, are for the smooth and safe functioning of society. After this huge crisis, I cannot see how we could go back to the previous "normal." We have used this lockdown time to cultivate new ways of communication and working, and new community relationships. We need to create a "new normal" where we reinvent our planet as a sustainable world. There is no Planet B. We have been able to change our ways very quickly to combat this deadly pandemic. We can do it again to preserve our world, for ourselves and for future generations.

—*Alicia Merrett*
Wells, Somerset, United Kingdom

Lynn Hanna, *Forced Change*, 53 × 46 in.
Photo: Michael Graves

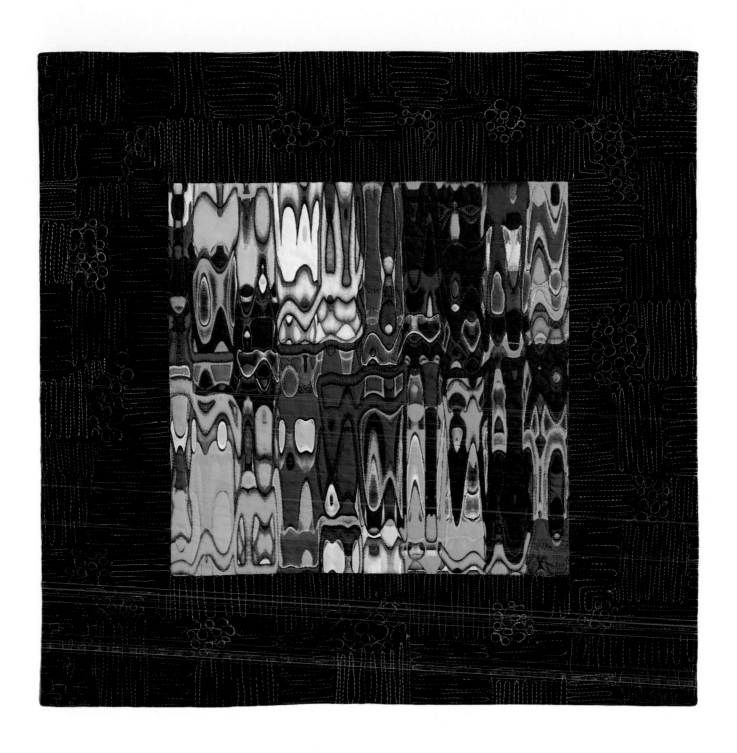

Alicia Merrett, *Up and Down and Round and Round*, 29 × 29 in.

Elisabeth Nacenta de la Croix, *Marée Arctique: de glace et d'eau (Arctic Tides: of Ice and Water)*, 49 × 20 in.
Photo: Olivier Junod

Giovanna Nicolai, *Emozioni altalenanti (Mood Swings)*, 28 × 24 in.

The arctic zone is constantly changing with the modification of the temperatures every year higher than the previous one. Since many years now, I feel greatly concerned by the impact our way of life has on certain areas of the globe. This quilt is about the melting of the icebergs, and its long and narrow shape speaks of the height of the icebergs and the broken quilted lines express the unfortunately expected break of one huge iceberg into several smaller ones. I made this work during the COVID lockdown in the spring of 2020, when I was feeling very happy to have so much time to devote to creativity. Then as weeks passed by, I was very down, doing nothing as lockdown seemed to last forever.

—*Elisabeth Nacenta de la Croix*
Geneva, Switzerland

This quilt, created during the lockdown, represents a moment of strong stress when the mood changes many times throughout the day. Crazy pieces bring you up and down with them in a continuous swing, from hope to desperation.

—*Giovanna Nicolai*
Mestre-Venice, Italy

The COVID 19 pandemic effectively labeled the necessities of life into two categories: "essential" and "nonessential." Purchase of my fabric necessities came into question: Could my home stash keep me going? Did I have enough yardage to finish a quilt back? Being a dedicated quilter, I normally enjoy a bit of sewing between my daily responsibilities, and now my supply chain was under threat. I decided to be resourceful with my quilting supplies: all the fabric for my next project would be curated from my scrap bin, a tightly stuffed plastic clothes hamper. Without consideration of color or print, my criterion for scrap-fabric selection was that they be large enough for my double-wedding-ring templates designed by Victoria Findlay Wolfe—if the template covered it, I cut it out! From that scrappy pile, I stuck pieces on my design wall that contained patterns of high contrast and colors that drew my eyes around the composition. Once I liked the arrangement, I began piecing the blocks.

—*Corinne Pitcher*
Oceanside, California, USA

While sheltering at home, I made my quilt entirely from fabric scraps curated from past quilts and clothing. Since it was safer to stay inside, all the material was what I had on hand. The color palette is weighted and somber with pops of color representing creativity and hope. The quilting is dense, and changes color. The binding is also pieced from fabrics in my stash.

—*Stephanie Zacharer Ruyle*
Denver, Colorado, USA

Corinne Pitcher, *Quarantine 2020 Scrap Quilt*, 57 × 57 in.
Photo: Gwen G. Long

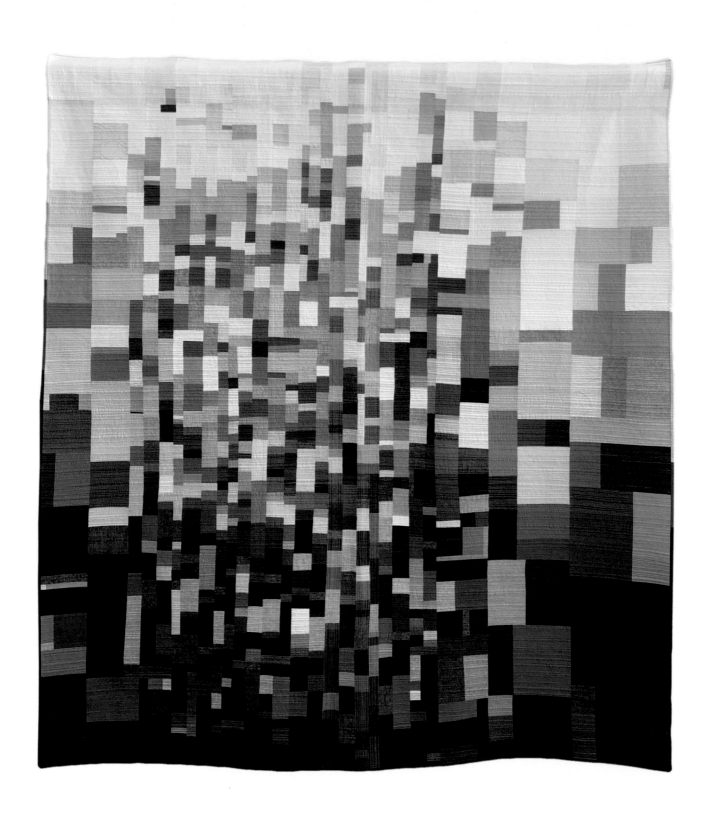

Stephanie Zacharer Ruyle, *Humble Beginnings*, 66 × 58 in.

Kelly Spell, *Stay in Your Log Cabin*, 27 × 27 in.

I began making tiny Log Cabin blocks on March 16, a few days after much of the United States went into lockdown. I found comfort in the familiarity of a traditional quilt design. Through the monotonous assembly of more than 2,600 logs, I was able to exert a small amount of control over the chaos and uncertainly of this new pandemic life. The dots on the pink fabric represent people isolating at home—or not, as it turned out. When I finished my quilt at the end of June, the celebratory feeling I usually experience after completing a quilt was absent. Perhaps that's because although my quilt is done, the pandemic is far from over.

—Kelly Spell
Hixson, Tennessee, USA

February 2020: Our daughter works at a hospital; tells us about a virus now known as COVID-19. I'm working with hand-appliquéd blocks in blue and white, and machine-pieced blocks in red and white.

March 2020: Our son calls. Our twenty-eight-year-old grandson is in an emergency room, needing heart surgery. While twenty-five or so family members wait more than half a day in hospital to hear if the surgery was successful, I set up a table in the waiting room to work on my quilt. I also prayed for my grandson and the surgeons.

Several days later: Pandemic stay-at-home orders for Arizona. Saddened and thinking of all first responders.

Days later: Sister-in-law calls. My husband's brother passed away. We were unable to say our good-byes.

April 2020: I'm not feeling well, am exhausted, stressed, and have a dry cough. My husband and I are tested for COVID-19. I test positive and my husband does not.

Four days later, our son calls. His daughter, our oldest granddaughter, has given birth to a baby boy. That makes two girls and a boy for their family. Quarantine has kept us away and we cannot see the baby. I'm now working on his baby quilt.

Everything now fits perfectly in my quarantine quilt design. Red fabrics in blocks known as Red Cross represent firefighters. Blue fabrics in blocks known as Orange Peel represent police officers. White background fabric represents all medical workers. With the help of my husband, we created a border design: tears of sadness for all lives lost, tears of happiness for all lives saved, and tears of joy for all lives born during this time of quarantine.

—Mary Andra Holmes
Prescott, Arizona, USA

OPPOSITE: Mary Andra Holmes, *First Responders*, 75 × 67.5 in.
Quilted by Andee Andriole.
Photo: Maryann Conner

"[A]n isolation full of sublimity; a freedom which the attached can never know."

—VIRGINIA WOOLF, *Mrs. Dalloway*

CHAPTER FIVE

Pandemic Landscapes

During quarantine, what we can see out of our windows and doorways has become disproportionately important. My spirit uplifted when trees budded with the soft green of spring. Unlike other summers, with the noise of visitors and lots of movement in our house and on the deck, this year we have become more appreciative of our wildlife visitors that show up often and keep us company—birds, chipmunks, squirrels, deer—(well, not the skunks). Views from quarantine in this chapter include an abstract cityscape by Anne Bellas, and Bobbi Baugh's sketches from her porch.

Other artists depicted imaginary landscapes, nostalgia for a favorite but distant locale, and even an undersea scene. Margaret Abramshe's ghostlike figures in Central Park capture the incredibly sad emptiness of Manhattan this year during springtime. Jeanne Marklin's quilt reminds us of courageous workers, such as firefighters, who continue their service while risking exposure to COVID-19. This chapter also presents two very different landscapes: Maria Billings's isolation in the California mountains, and Taiwanese artist Hsiu-Pei Hsieh's optimistic, sun-filled park scene of the future, where most people are now immune or have been vaccinated, with only a few having to wear a protective face mask.

Artists' Narratives

The scene is of Central Park filled with shadow figures—a young family, a worker trimming the trees, a jogger, and an elderly couple. The composition is designed to express loss. Both the loss of the individual and the loss for the community. Flying above the figures are a series of cranes. Cranes are a symbol of happiness, longevity, and good fortune. They are placed in the composition to assure the viewer that the future still holds our hope.

—*Margaret Abramshe*
St. George, Utah, USA

This quilt is largely autobiographical. But what visual and symbolic language would tell the story? During quarantine, I gave myself hours to sit on the porch in the evening to think, to sketch, to write. I used time in the studio simply looking and absorbing the images as I created them. Some parts of the work came quickly. Some did not. Pandemic days colored by the mood of chaos beyond my walls suited the emotional process. Two girls wearing their look-at-us-being-good dresses are in a place of dream and memory. Things are juxtaposed unexpectedly. A fairy-tale forest. Tradition. Home. Passages. Work. Societal expectations. The girls' job is to figure out the meaning of it all.

—*Bobbi Baugh*
DeLand, Florida, USA

This lockdown time caused many of us to create and fight the gloomy situation. I myself quilted nearly half a dozen art quilts reflecting the times, my feelings, the essentials of our lives, the possibility of dreams. It was nurturing and soothing to quilt.

—*Anne Bellas*
Nantes, France

OPPOSITE: Margaret Abramshe, *Ghost Town*, 42 × 31 in.

Bobbi Baugh, *What Were We Supposed to Be?*, 39 × 120 in.

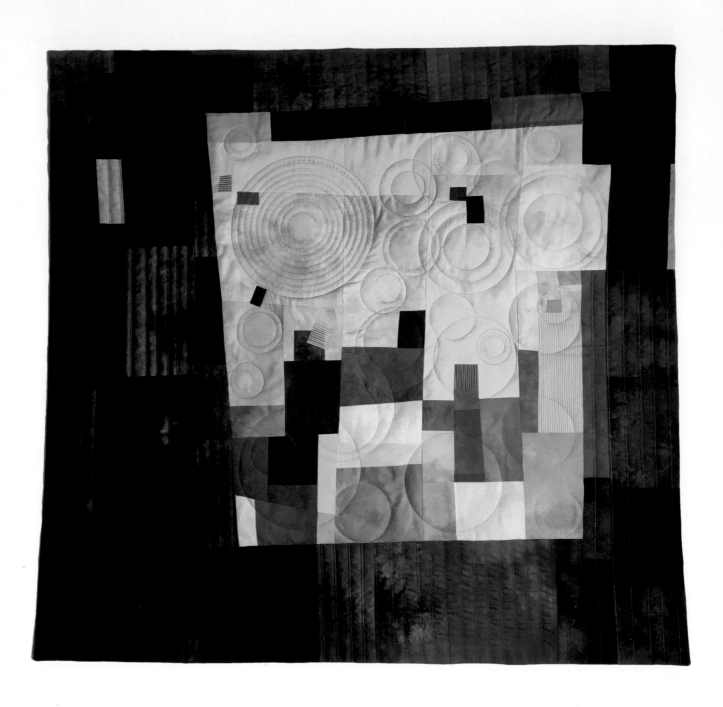

Anne Bellas, *Quarantined: View from My Window*, 51 × 49 in.

Week 2 of lockdown: A highly esteemed in-law grandma died of COVID-19 in Geneva, Switzerland. She was in great form, planning for her one hundredth birthday party in May. (The city of Geneva offers its centenarians this party.) Then two or three days with the virus and she passed away in her sleep. Week 2 also brought a poison-oak infection on my chin, neck, both hands, and wrists: time to think about my next textile painting. Week 5 of lockdown brought two friends from New York City into our household. After leaving the sirens and difficulties of New York, they self-quarantined for two weeks and then joined us. It's quite a lively household now. They are so grateful. It's almost a little embarrassing, but that's what friends are for: you ask for help and you get it. Maybe in the future a person not yet born will ask: "How was this time of isolation and quarantine?" I'd like to leave a visual answer in the form of my textile painting *Isolation in the California Coastal Range*.

—*Maria Billings*
Oregon House, California, USA

Maria Billings, *Isolation in the California Coastal Range*, 20 × 40 in.

Jeanne Marklin, *Burning Up*, 33 × 44 in.

I was working on this quilt during the first couple of months of being isolated. It had me wondering if the heating-up of the planet could be affecting the spread or activation of the virus. Seeing the skies clearing up while people were quarantined made me think of the environmental impact of being isolated and wondering if there might be a positive result. Or if there will once again be awful forest fires in Australia and the West.

—Jeanne Marklin
Williamstown, Massachusetts, USA

I live in Lucca, in the Tuscany region of Italy. Lucca is an awesomely beautiful Renaissance town between Pisa and Florence. Like all Italian towns during the height of the pandemic, Lucca was a ghost town. No one left homes unless it was to go for groceries or medications, and then only with an official government form stating why and where you were going. Life was surreal, primarily because of fear of the unknown and for concern about our friends and family. I lived most of my life in the US, most recently in New Mexico after working for thirty years in Washington, DC. I moved to Lucca in 2018 and I absolutely love my life here. I was surprised to discover a rich quilting community, which has inspired me to continue with my art quilts. Sadly, during the Italian pandemic lockdown, I had a constant sense of stress knowing there was so much death and loss of livelihood surrounding me. I knew that I needed something that could bring positive thoughts and beauty to my life. I had a photograph from a recent visit to a seaside village in Cinque Terre on the Mediterranean coast of Italy. Looking at that photograph reminded me of the beauty and good life that I hoped would return. I decided to focus my energy on creating an art quilt that incorporated that image. With each addition of color and with each stitch, I felt a renewed sense of happiness with a promise of a positive future. As we say in Italy, *andrà tutto bene*, everything will be OK.

—Roderick Daniel
Lucca, Italy

Roderick Daniel, *Cinque Terre*, 36 × 30 in.
Photo: Jim Carnevale

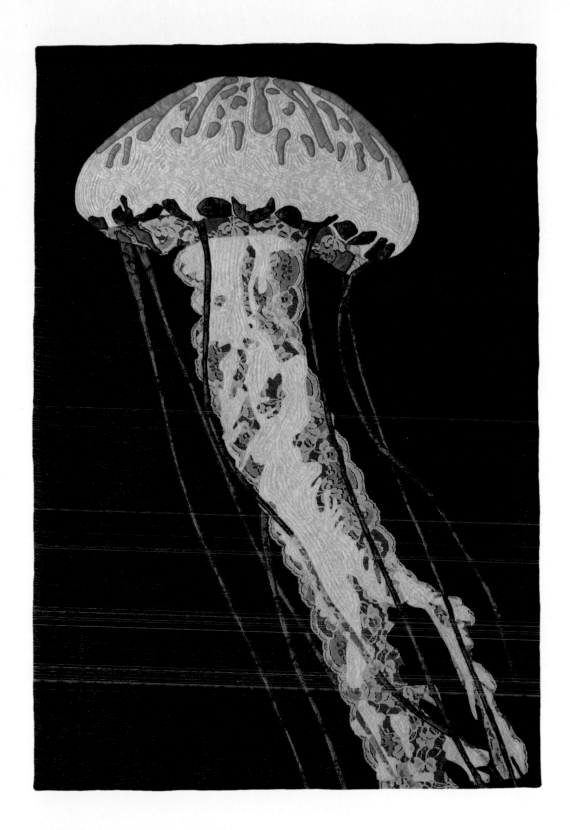

Laurie Mutalipassi, *Midnight Swim*, 36 × 24 in.
Photo: Johanna Love

Hsiu-Pei Hsieh, *Embrace the Future*, 43 × 54 in.

Even when a storm is raging over the ocean, this jellyfish swims in the ocean's calm, deep waters. This reminds us that when dealing with chaos caused by coronavirus, we can react calmly and wisely. If we dig deep into our emotional strength, we too can "swim" calmly through the coronavirus waters. (Inspiration photo by Phillip Colla.)

—Laurie Mutalipassi
Westminster, California, USA

Due to the coronavirus outbreak, we need to wear masks, keep our social distance, and even self-quarantine at home. However, this too shall pass. Let us look forward and embrace the future.

— Hsiu-Pei Hsieh
Taoyuan City, Taiwan

"Loneliness clarifies. Here silence stands Like heat."

—PHILIP LARKIN,
"Here"

CHAPTER SIX

Politics and Protest

From coast to coast and on to Australia, dismay and dissatisfaction with governmental response to COVID-19 and to racial turmoil informs this chapter. The year 2020 began with excitement over the one hundredth anniversary of the Nineteenthth Amendment to the US Constitution by which women finally won the right to vote in national elections—even though that celebratory event brought its own racial tensions since, in practice, suffrage in this country extended mostly to white women. Alice Beasley's quilt dramatically addresses this issue.

Many of the celebrations planned for the one hundredth anniversary have been canceled because of the pandemic. Somewhat ironically, the original Suffrage Movement in this country was sidelined by the 1918 pandemic, which lasted well into 1919. An article by Alisha Haridasani Gupta published April 28, 2020, in the *New York Times* explained how lockdowns and cancellation of suffragist rallies contributed to the Nineteenth Amendment not passing in 1918, especially since some of the suffragist leaders themselves were ill. But today we have a powerful tool not available in 1918 for political activism, and we have seen how the internet has helped spearhead social-justice initiatives and document racial oppression.

As for the failings of numerous government leaders around the world to react in a timely manner to the coronavirus, we can only hope that the seriousness of the COVID-19 contagion is now obvious to everyone. By the time this book is published in late spring of 2021, we can only hope that the coronavirus has been contained, a vaccine has been provided for everyone, and in the future the world will be better prepared.

Artists' Narratives

A lot of my work is about the intersection of race and politics in America. I was invited to make this quilt for an exhibition commemorating the one hundredth anniversary of women's suffrage scheduled to open at the Clinton Presidential Library after the COVID-19 threat abates. This piece calls out the moment when Ida B. Wells and her delegation of black women suffragists from Chicago were told they would not be allowed to march with the other Illinois women in the 1913 suffrage parade in Washington, DC. They could either walk at the tail end (behind the men) or not at all, a dictate that Wells declined. The title of my quilt comes from black feminist scholar Anna Julia Cooper, who rebutted the assumption that white women could dictate the place of black women in the Suffragist Movement, stating "only the black woman can say 'when and where I enter, in the quiet, undisputed dignity of my womanhood.'" I finished this piece while sheltered in place in my studio. The irony of depicting white privilege one hundred years ago was not lost on me as I watched armed white men marching to claim their constitutional right to a haircut and to drink in bars in reckless disregard of my right as a senior-citizen black woman to live and vote in safety. Then, just as the last stitches were being made in my quilt, a white policeman chose to kneel on the neck of George Floyd for nine minutes. It was as if the hand that reaches out in my piece to taunt Ida B. Wells continues to wag at black people a hundred years later; to say your rights, your very lives, are still only at the sufferance of whites.

—Alice Beasley
Oakland, California, USA

Alice Beasley, *"When and Where I Enter,"* 44 × 70 in.
Photo: Sibila Savage Photography

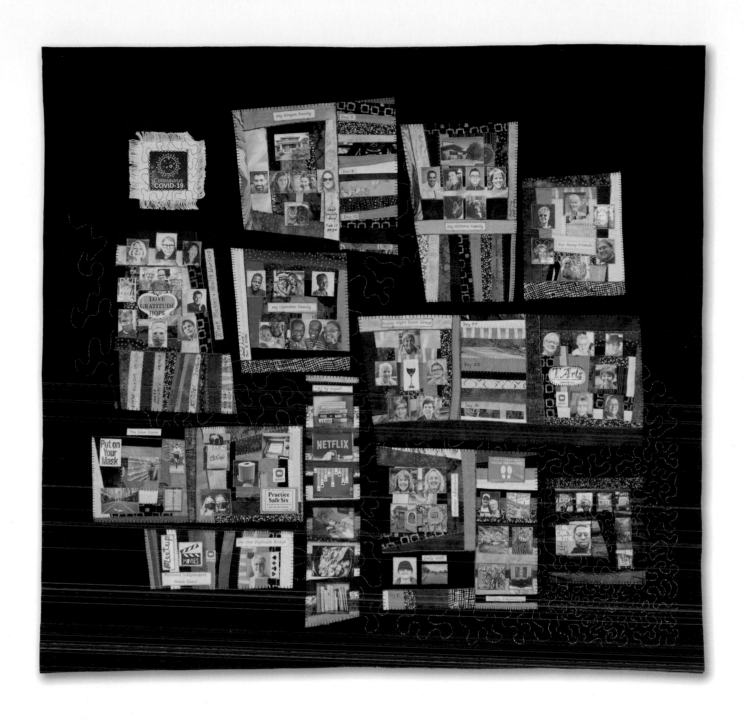

OPPOSITE: Michael A. Cummings, *Shirley Chisholm*, 85 × 75 in.
Photo: Torrey Coates

Jo Noble, *Picking Up the Pieces*, 40 × 43 in.
Photo: Sam Q. Garnett

Like Alice Beasley, I was invited to make this quilt for the Clinton Presidential Library exhibition. I started construction in February and finished in late April, after researching information about Shirley Chisholm. After I collected a number of facts, read her book, and selected her quotes, I started to visualize my ideas, thinking of vintage campaign posters and how decorative they were with American flags and campaign slogans. Adding state flags to my borders provided the perfect Americana element. I also had to block out events happening around me. I reside in New York City, and was living in the epicenter of the pandemic. It was the first exposure to the coronavirus in the US. There were so many unknown facts and it was so easy to be infected. We had to quarantine ourselves. As statistics mounted, fear and anxiety increased in me and the entire city. I am in a high-risk group due to age and asthma, so I was terrified. Some nights in bed I had anxiety attacks, thinking I had a fever, when it was only too much cover. Looking at the news on television about bodies piling up because hospitals and funeral homes had no space, and refrigerator trucks were storing bodies, I escaped from the news by working on this quilt. There is some degree of stress whenever I go outside. I avoid crowds if I go out. I have not seen my friends and don't know when I will be able to go to visit my elderly mother in California. This quilt was a great distraction from all the pain, suffering, and loss taking place in my city.

—*Michael A. Cummings*
New York, New York, USA

Scraps from masks were gathered together to become the current blocks of my life. Where our lives were once fluid, we now live more isolated, more restricted. COVID-19 floats around my life, but so too does the promise of social justice. Black Lives Matter. Rest in peace, George Floyd, and all who have gone before and are still affected. We are watching, listening, and acting.

—*Jo Noble*
Portland, Oregon, USA

At his Tulsa rally, Donald Trump bragged he had told his people to slow down the testing for COVID-19. When confronted, he claimed he was joking, a typical gaslighter response. Imagine the commander in chief joking about his orders to decrease testing when more than 120,000 people have died.

—*Mel Dugosh*
Hondo, Texas, USA

Mel Dugosh, *Gaslighter in Chief*, 44 × 36 in.

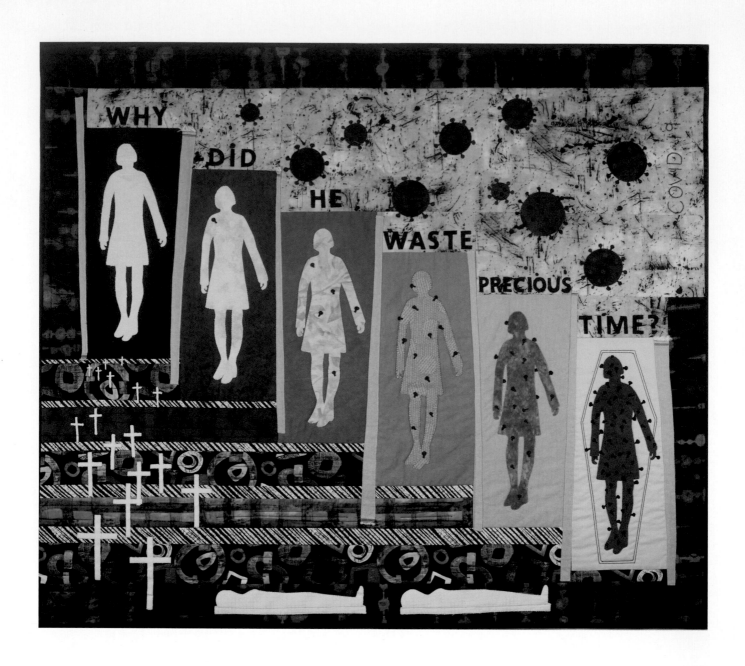

Sue Rasmussen, *DENIAL*, 35 × 40 in.

Quarantine forced upon me days and days of little contact or interaction with other people, and so I spent more time than ever watching news broadcasts, listening with alarm to the growing pandemic situation and the ineptitude of our government to handle it. The demands of self-isolation, however, allowed me to recognize and focus on my feelings of frustration and anger, and to listen to my heart, filled with dismay as illnesses increased daily, and to recognize our collective fear of this unknown killer. I awoke one morning with this idea for a quilt after listening to the disturbing news that President Trump had indeed been briefed on the COVID-19 pandemic in early January and February 2020, and that he had done nothing to initiate or coordinate a plan to combat this disease. His denial and lies wasted precious time, causing countless unnecessary deaths and illness. I felt compelled to embroider my feelings in the borders: Quarantine, Loneliness, Doubt, Distancing, Anxiety, Fear, Death, Denial. This quilt is a tribute to all those frontline first responders—the nurses, doctors, hospital workers, EMTs, paramedics—represented by a woman in this quilt—who selflessly worked day after day in harm's way to save lives. It is dedicated to those responders who have died to save others.

—*Sue Rasmussen*
Simi Valley, California, USA

Eyes are remarkable organs. The sensory membrane of the retina contains millions of light-sensitive photoreceptor cells that receive and organize visual information and send signals onto the brain for visual recognition. As we survey the world, the COVID-19 pandemic has been challenging to process. It seems like we are constantly recalibrating perceptions to accommodate the new normal. The outlook is increasingly suffused with zemblanity—making unhappy, unlucky, and expected surprises occurring by design—the opposite of serendipity. Sheer unrelenting pandemic metrics bring unpleasant nonsurprises, both socially and economically. It goes beyond mere spectatorship because our lives have been materially altered.

—*Brenda Gael Smith*
Copacabana, New South Wales, Australia

OPPOSITE: Brenda Gael Smith, *Acuity #5: Zemblanity*, 68 × 52 in.

Julie Haddrick, *Kintsukuroi Illuminated*, 39 × 39 in.

Kintsukuroi is the Japanese art of mending broken ceramics, also known as the Golden Mend. The great pride given to repairing broken pottery with resin and gold emphasizes both break and mend. Like *wabi sabi* where the flawed, aged, or imperfect is embraced, *kintsukuroi* pottery is deemed more beautiful for having been broken. The concept of illuminated repair holds deep psychological significance during the COVID-19 pandemic as we focus on mending everything that has been broken.

—Julie Haddrick
Adelaide, South Australia, Australia

The fact that we were all forced to stay at home was a strange but not uncomfortable directive for me. Secretly I was not unhappy (aside from the health standpoint). I am a homebody and love being in my studio and creating. Now everyone was in the same place and could not lure me out with invitations for lunch, canasta, and get-togethers. I worked on *We Are All . . . Hanging by a Thread* slowly for two months since I had nowhere to go and no pressure to be anywhere. The theme became how we are each so distinctive and divergent but must endeavor to get along to survive. The layers of fabrics on each square represent the depth of individual personalities. The threads are our connectors, as each thread shows how delicate and tenuous our relationships can be. These threads alone are thin and vulnerable, but together each stitch strengthens and builds on the next for the durability of the art, just as in relationships and communities for the greater good of the world. For me, those threads tangled and hanging represent how communication can sometimes be so stressful. We need each other to survive and our differences are paramount for that continuity. Diversity creates opportunity for a society to grow in character, education, and social norms, and to allow our humanity to prosper.

—Nancy Billings
Miami, Florida, USA

OPPOSITE: Nancy Billings, *We Are All . . . Hanging by a Thread*, 55 × 45 in.
Photo: Fabrizio Cacciatore

I made this quilt out of frustration with the federal government's lack of response to COVID-19. Essential workers and healthcare workers have gone above and beyond. The rest of us stayed home, worked from home while caring for and homeschooling our children, and socially distanced ourselves from friends and loved ones. We did our part so the government could do theirs, and they did nothing, while loudly congratulating themselves, and then reopened far too soon.

—*Tamara King*
Portland, Oregon, USA

"You'd think that time stood still, it moves so slowly; with lagging steps the year pursues its way. . . . Or does universal time run its usual course, and only for my harsh life does time stand still?"

—Ovid,
Lamentations [poems written from exile, trans. Stephen Hinds]

OPPOSITE: Tamara King, *This Is Bullshit*, 47 × 29 in.

INDEX OF ARTISTS

Sandra Sider, *Dandelion: Tough as the Tooth of a Lion*, 44 × 40 × 5 in.
(floor installation with vinyl backing)